Law and Society
Recent Scholarship

Edited by Melvin I. Urofsky

A Series from LFB Scholarly

Oral Argument and Amicus Curiae

Matthew M.C. Roberts

LFB Scholarly Publishing LLC
El Paso 2012

Library of Congress Cataloging-in-Publication Data

Roberts, Matthew M.C., 1976-
Oral argument and amicus curiae / Matthew M.C. Roberts.
p. cm. -- (Law & society : recent scholarship)
Includes bibliographical references and index.
ISBN 978-1-59332-466-7 (hardcover : alk. paper)
1. United States. Supreme Court--Decision making. 2. Amici curiae--United States. 3. Forensic orations--United States. 4. Political questions and judicial power--United States. 5. Public interest law--United States. I. Title.
KF8748.R63 2012
347.73'26--dc23

2011036551

ISBN 978-1-59332-466-7

Printed on acid-free 250-year-life paper.

Manufactured in the United States of America.

Table of Contents

List of Tables

List of Figures

Acknowledgements

I owe a great debt to Tim Johnson. As an undergraduate, I loved politics in the abstract. It was only after I arrived at grad school that I found an object for my affection: the judiciary. Courses in judicial process and constitutional law hooked me, but it was Tim's seminar on the Supreme Court in American Life that showed me why courts are empirically fascinating. Courts, like mushrooms, seem to do best in the dark. They work mostly in secret, shielded from the light that tries to flood other branches of government. And yet the vital role they play in our politics makes understanding judicial decision-making not only an empirical challenge but also a democratic necessity. With Tim's gracious consent, this conviction helped take a co-authored paper and turned it into the book before you.

Thanks are also due to the numerous conference discussants and colleagues who have weighed-in on portions of this research. I fear that any remaining flaws contained within belong solely to the author.

Finally, I am deeply indebted to my family for their continuing support, especially my long-suffering wife Kristen, without whom this project would never have been possible.

—MMCR

CHAPTER 1

Listening to Friends

A TALE OF TWO CASES

Louisiana

On Wednesday April16, 2008, the Supreme Court heard arguments in the case of *Kennedy v. Louisiana*. Even though the Court had recently decided two high profile death penalty cases—*Atkins v. Virginia* (536 U.S. 304, 2002) and *Roper v. Simmons* (543 U.S. 551, 2005)—this latest case would address a different wrinkle in capital punishment. Some thirty years earlier in *Coker v. Georgia* (433 U.S. 584, 1977), the Court had ruled that the death penalty was not a suitable punishment for rape. Held to be out of proportion with the crime in question, capital punishment became effectively, if not explicitly, confined to instances involving the loss of human life. Although the facts of the case and the justices' opinion referred narrowly to the rape of an adult woman, the holdings and dicta in *Coker* left unclear whether capital punishment would be permissible for the rape of a child.

In 1995, the state of Louisiana enacted a law that allowed the imposition of the death penalty for the rape of a child under the age of twelve. The first test of the law's constitutionality would begin in 1998, when Patrick Kennedy called 911. In the call and in his subsequent testimony to authorities, Kennedy maintained that he found his eight year old stepdaughter shortly after she had been raped by two neighborhood boys. The girl described the same sequence of events—at least initially. When her story began to change and details of the account began to unravel, the police turned their attention to Kennedy.[1]

The case finally went to trial some five years later. The prosecution depended successfully on the victim's own testimony and Kennedy was found guilty of the aggravated rape of a child. The jury unanimously agreed on the sentence: death. Two factors seemed to seal this outcome. First was the horrific nature of the assault itself, the details of which are best left to the Court's opinion. Second was the testimony of another female family member who reported that Kennedy had also sexually abused her on three separate occasions when she was eight years old. With little factual basis for disputing his conviction, Kennedy's appeals centered on the lingering uncertainty about capital punishment for the rape of a minor. Louisiana's own Supreme Court upheld the conviction and sentence. *Coker's* silence on the issue was not dispositive, the court argued. Instead, they held that the uniquely vulnerable status of children warranted an increased attention to deterrence and retribution for such crimes. The court also distinguished Kennedy's situation from that of other death penalty cases heard by the Supreme Court, in which diminished culpability invalidated capital punishment.[2]

The United States Supreme Court granted certiorari on January 4, 2008. As could have been predicted from the case's high profile, a variety of interest groups sought to participate in the case as *amici curiae*. Of the seven briefs filed by outside interests, five of them supported Kennedy. Some of the arguments were familiar criticisms of the death penalty and the criminal justice system overall. The Louisiana Association of Criminal Defense Lawyers and the Louisiana Public Defenders Association pointed out the overburdened defense system for indigents which was unprepared to offer the quality of counsel necessary for cases involving capital punishment. The National Association of Criminal

---

[1] Certain aspects of the story must certainly have been suspicious, such as the petitioner's description of one of the assailant's bicycles, which matched a bike found behind a nearby apartment—albeit one whose tires were flat, which lacked gears, and which was covered in spider webs. The most damning evidence, though, must have been the phone calls Kennedy made a full ninety minutes before he called 911. In one he asked a coworker for help on removing blood from white carpeting. In another call he asked a carpet cleaning company for urgent assistance in removing bloodstains from carpet (128 S. Ct. 2646–7).

[2] See *Atkins v. Virginia* (536 U.S. 304, 2002) invalidating capital punishment for the mentally handicapped, and *Roper v. Simmons* (543 U.S. 551, 2005) invalidating it for defendants under the age of 18.

Defense Lawyers worried about the fact that child rape cases so often depend upon the unsupported and unreliable testimony of minors. The ACLU detailed the racially discriminatory history of the death penalty. A group of British attorneys, judges, and legal scholars filed a brief which discussed that nation's elimination of death as a punishment for rape. Finally, the National Association of Social Workers proposed a number of arguments, including the theory that allowing the death penalty for child rape makes offenders more likely to kill their victims.

Louisiana was not alone on its side of the case. A brief filed by the governor of Missouri and members of its General Assembly, and one filed by the attorneys general of nine separate states, laid out the claims for adopting capital punishment in the face of the Court's ambiguity. Missouri was actually in the process of drafting such legislation when the Court heard the Kennedy case. Part of the state's brief rested on the claim that by deciding in the petitioner's favor, the Court would be foreclosing the nation's deliberation on the issue of the death penalty.

While *amici* for Kennedy outnumbered those for Louisiana more than two-to-one, the state had what should have been an unusual advantage. Approximately one month before the case was to be argued, Texas filed a motion with the Court for divided argument—the opportunity for an *amicus* to appear with their party at oral arguments. While such requests are not unheard of, the fact that the Court granted it is out of the ordinary. Between 1953 and 1985, the years covered by James Gibson's United States Supreme Court Judicial Database, only eight percent of cases had an oral *amicus*.

R. Edward Cruz, the Texas Solicitor General who argued for the state as *amicus*, was a graduate of Harvard Law, a former clerk for Chief Justice Rehnquist, a six time veteran of argument before the Court, and the recipient of multiple awards from the National Association of Attorneys General.[3] Cruz's argument reflects his extensive experience. Compared to the Louisiana district attorney he argued with, Cruz was a model of confidence, deftly answering the justices' questions without becoming flustered. Within the first minutes of his argument he corrected an important factual error that the justices had introduced and which the Louisiana attorney had failed to point out. During his brief time at the podium he also managed to weave together insightful comments on two of the major themes dealt with during the argu-

[3] For preliminary reflections on the success of state attorneys general as *amici* before the Supreme Court, please see Nicholson 2009.

ment with the other attorneys: the question of how to narrow the criteria for which rapes deserve the death penalty, and the question of how to discern a national trend on the issue of capital punishment for the rape of a child.

Washington

Four years prior to the events of *Kennedy*, another tragic tale unfolded on the other side of the country. It all began on May 23, 1991. Cal Coburn Brown was a thirty-five year-old parolee who had been in an Oregon prison on a prior assault charge.[4] When a planned visit to a former girlfriend in Seattle turned sour, Brown found himself in need of cash. He approached the car of Holly Washa, a native of Nebraska who had recently moved to the area. After getting her to open her car door by suggesting there was a problem with her tire, Brown forced his way into the car and threatened Washa with a knife. Over the next thirty-six hours Brown forced her to withdraw money from her bank account and had her forge checks from her roommates' accounts. He ultimately brought her back to a motel room, where she had earlier been bound and gagged. Washa was raped and brutally tortured before being placed in the trunk of her car. Brown slashed her and strangled her before driving her car to a Park and Ride lot where he paid for six days of parking. After killing Washa, Brown boarded a flight for California where two days later, he similarly attacked another woman who managed to survive. After being caught and questioned by the California authorities, Brown admitted to the Washington killing.

Brown pled guilty to the California charges and was sentenced to life in prison. The state of Washington, though, sought the death penalty. It was the result of that trial, in which Brown was found guilty and sentenced to death, that prompted the case which would find its way to the Supreme Court. Brown's conviction was upheld by the Washington Supreme Court in 1997. His attorneys subsequently filed a federal habeas petition that alleged, among other things, that jury selection in the Washington trial had been unfairly manipulated to guarantee a death sentence instead of the alternative, life without parole. While the district court for the Western District of Washington denied Brown's peti-

---

[4] Brown's record stretched back into the 1970s when he held a woman at knifepoint in a California shopping mall. The charge that had him in the Oregon prison sprang from a 1984 incident where he broke into a woman's home and began to strangle her in the process of an attempted rape.

tion, the Ninth Circuit Court of Appeals granted it and reversed the decision, ordering a new sentencing trial for Brown.

The case of *Uttecht v. Brown* (551 U.S. 1) revolved around a dismissed juror, identified as Juror Z in the opinions and as Richard Deal in the oral argument. The principal issues of the case circulated around him: why the prosecutor chose to challenge Deal and other jurors, why defense counsel did or did not object to challenged jurors, whether the trial judge properly concluded the juror would be unable to serve, and whether the state and federal appellate courts gave proper deference under existing law and precedent.

Four *amicus* briefs were filed in the case. On Brown's side were briefs from the American Civil Liberties Union and the National Association of Criminal Defense Lawyers. On behalf of Uttecht, the Superintendent of the Washington State Penitentiary, was a brief from the state of Oregon, signed by twenty-two other states, and a brief from the Solicitor General's office. The latter would go on to petition the Court for time at oral argument, which the justices granted.

Attorneys for both parties faced stiff questioning. John J. Samson, Assistant Attorney General for Washington and counsel for petitioner, was especially pressed on how much could be read into the juror's ambiguous answers to voir dire, and whether deference to the trial court's silence on Deal's demeanor effectively eliminated the possibility of judicial review. Suzanne Lee Elliott, court-appointed counsel for the defense, received similar questions. Justices who ended up on both sides of the final decision were particularly interested in her explanation for why the defense had failed to object to the dismissal of Deal. Elliott tried to make clear that Washington law did not require such objections, and that questions of juror dismissal could be raised on appeal without an objection on the record.[5] For many of the justices, though, it was the failure to object which prevented the trial judge from making a specific finding about the reason for Deal's dismissal—essentially prompting the whole question of how much deference should be given to a cold and silent record.

---

[5] This failure to object was clearly a concern for members of the final majority: Kennedy, Roberts, Alito, Scalia, and Thomas. During Elliott's questioning, Justice Stevens also weighed-in on the issue, noting that the failure to object was one of the most troubling parts of the case. While Stevens still dissented in the case, he also did not sign onto Justice Breyer's opinion which explicitly argued that the failure to object was irrelevant.

The federal government's *amicus* brief noted in its statement of interest that their concern was with the case's implications for federal capital trials. This differentiation between state and federal cases was never raised during argument, however, because Deputy Solicitor General Michael Dreeben managed to speak only nine words before being interrupted by Justice Stevens, who explicitly asked the government attorney to pick-up where Washington's counsel left off.[6] Like Samson, Dreeben was forced to repeatedly defend the trial judge. While the former's time before the bench can hardly be characterized as a failure, Dreeben provided a level of detail that co-counsel had not. Responding in particular to questions from Justice Stevens, was able to demonstrate from the record that the trial judge had been both conscientious and demonstrably fair during the voir dire. When the defense posed objections to the prosecution's challenges of jurors, the judge made detailed findings to support the instances where he had dismissed the juror. He had also been more than generous in supporting the defense, upholding five out of the seven objections the defense had made. These revelations appear to have been important for demonstrating that the defense's failure to object to juror Deal had the effect of obfuscating the record for appellate review.

A Study in Contrasts

Despite the additional assistance that Cruz provided during argument in *Kennedy v. Louisiana*, the Court still ruled in Kennedy's favor and eliminated the ambiguity found in the earlier *Coker* decision. By contrast, in *Uttecht,* the side supported by an oral *amicus* won in the end. That any two cases should come out differently is not surprising in and of itself. Two things, however, make these cases an interesting contrast. Having an *amicus* share argument time is a fairly unusual deviation from the Court's normal routine, which should always arouse curiosity. What meaning can be ascribed to Cruz's presence, and what should be made of the fact that his argument appears not to have made a difference in the case? Did Cruz's presence potentially hurt Louisiana's case, instead of helping it as intended? Which is more typical—the experience in *Kennedy* or that in *Uttecht*? Can *amici* ever increase their influence on a case by appearing before the justices alongside the parties?

---

[6] Also interesting is that Dreeben faced intense questioning from every member of the Court's minority. Justice Kennedy asked two minor questions that essentially referred to those asked by other members of the Court.

Why, given the Court's limited resources, is there even such a thing as the oral *amicus*?

The second interesting contrast between the cases is the fact that the same Justice authored the majority opinion in both cases: Anthony Kennedy. While frequently seen as a member of the current Court's conservative wing, Kennedy is known for his tendency to act as a "swing voter" who often finds himself aligning with either side of the Court. What is it that leads a moderate justice to swing in the direction that he or she does? Could the somewhat unusual appearance of an *amicus* at oral argument play into that decision? To reach the answer to these questions, we should first consider what previous research has learned about friends of the court and oral arguments.

THE AMICUS CURIAE

In his seminal study of courts, Martin Shapiro notes that across societies, conflict resolution appears to be structured by the "logic of the triad"—two contesting parties relying upon a third-party decisionmaker (Shapiro 1986). One notable deviation from this standard is that of the *amicus curiae* (Barker 1967, 52–3). Stretching back to Roman legal tradition, third parties who are not actual litigants in a case may occasionally appear as "friends of the court" (Pfeffer 1981, 83; Angell 1967, 1017–8; see also Goldman 2011). To understand the original purpose of such appearances, one need look no farther than their use under English common law in the seventeenth and eighteenth centuries (Angell 1967, 1018). *Amici* were regularly given permission to appear before courts in order to: bring up relevant cases or statutes not known to the judge; point out "manifest error" in the case; inform the court of legislative intent; and to remedy defects in the adversarial process (Krislov 1963, 695–7). In short, *amici* provided the judicial system with neutral, unbiased information. Such assistance was welcomed because of the presumption that "it is for the honor of a court of justice to avoid error" (quoted in Krislov 1963, 695).

Even though the Attorney General was allowed to intervene in the 1812 admiralty suit *The Schooner Exchange v. McFadden*, the first true appearance of an *amicus curiae* in the United States Supreme Court came in the 1821 case of *Green v. Biddle* (Angell 1967, 1018; Krislov 1963, 698, 700). *Green* concerned federal supremacy and land holdings in the state of Kentucky, but was decided without any representation of Kentucky itself. Acting on behalf of the state, Henry Clay successfully petitioned for a rehearing and then was allowed to argue as *amicus*. Following Clay's appearance it became fairly common for the federal government, federal agencies, and states to participate as *amici* (Krislov 1963, 702). At the same time, the Court was also becoming more willing to accept the appearance of private citizens as *amici*, often when they were party to similar litigation still pending in lower courts (Krislov 1963, 703).

The rise of the American *amicus*, however, marked a departure from its previous uses. Krislov suggests that this change was seen most clearly in the way *amicus* briefs were signed. (Krislov 1963, 703). Traditionally the authoring attorney was viewed as the *amicus*, not the organization he represented. By the 1930's—long after the underlying change actually began—this emphasis on the professional role of the *amicus* was lost and briefs were openly identified with the sponsoring group. Instead of being truly neutral "friends of the court," *amici* are now seen as advocating particular case outcomes, usually in direct support of one litigant or the other.

The Court itself has remained generally supportive of the practice, perhaps because the justices think of *amici* as prospective future litigants or as the voice of other interests impacted by the Court's actions (Krislov 1963, 704). Starting in 1938, the Court began laying out formal rules to govern the *amicus* process, requiring potential *amici* to secure the written consent of all parties to the case (O'Connor and Epstein 1983, 37).[7] Subsequent changes in 1949 have required that groups still interested in participating after being denied consent by the parties must file a motion for leave to file, and in 1997 the Court required the disclosure of relationships between the parties and potential *amici* (O'Connor and Epstein 1983, 39; Kearney and Merrill 2000, 766).[8]

---

[7] The Court formally excludes from this requirement the Solicitor General, the federal government, and the states (O'Connor and Epstein 1983, 37).

[8] The question of how often *amici* and litigants' attorneys coordinate their activities (and whether doing so is wise) remains an open one. Writing in 1981, Pfeffer argued that because of filing deadlines, attorney pride, and practicality briefs *amicus* were generally prepared without having seen a given party's brief (Pfeffer 1981, 105). Foreshadowing Caldeira and Wright's 1988 article, Baker argues that attorney behavior is conditional; at the *certiorari* stage counsel for respondents should discourage *amici* while counsel for petitioner should recruit one good brief (Baker 1984, 626). McGuire argues that encouraging *amicus* involvement is a sign of attorney sophistication, and that sophisticated attorneys tend to have more success before the Court (McGuire 1994; McGuire

While the formal rules about *amicus* involvement could be useful to a Court that regularly complains about its workload, except for a period in the 1950's the justices have never purposefully limited the access that *amici* have to Court proceedings (O'Connor and Epstein 1983, 41; see also Frey 2006, 5; and Collins 2008, 42–5).

Regardless of neutrality or advocacy, *amici curiae* have been of fundamental interest to those studying Supreme Court decision-making. Long before the advent of the strategic model of decision making (c.f. Epstein and Knight 1998), conventional wisdom held almost *a priori* that friends of the court could have a discernable impact on the Court's decisions. Most agree that the heart of an *amicus'* influence comes from the provision of information (Barker 1967, 54). The Court itself hinted at such in the 1867 case known as *The Gray Jacket.* After allowing the Treasury Department to participate as an *amicus*, the Court justified its decision by saying that it was "desirous of all the light that can be derived from the fullest discussion" (quoted in Krislov 702; 72 U.S. 342 at 371).

Traditionally *amici* have been seen as providing courts with additional information not offered by the litigants themselves (Barker 1967, 53; Koshansky 1977, 8; Simmons 2009, 207). This may take the form of supplemental legal arguments or information about the impact of the Court's decision and the preferences of external actors (Barker 1967, 54, 56, 60; Pfeffer 1981, 107; Ennis 1984, 606, 608; Caldeira and Wright 1988, 1112; Epstein and Knight 1999, 215; Pacelle 2006, 317; Spriggs and Wahlbeck 1997, 367–8; Collins 2004, 808; Frey 2006). Baker argues, for example, that *amici* can more safely argue for overruling precedent than can the parties (Baker 1984, 626). At times *amici* might introduce factual or scientific data believed to be necessary for the Court's decision (Roesch et al. 1991; Koshansky 1977, 13–4). Collins has found that third party briefs almost always provide new legal authorities beyond those identified by the parties (Collins 2008, 66).

Not all the information presented by *amici* need be entirely new. When authoring briefs, parties find themselves limited in many ways—most notably in their ability to cover a large number of points given the Court's imposed page limitations. *Amici*, though also constrained by page limitations, may choose to focus on just one or two of a party's

---

1995). Drawing upon interviews with previous clerks, Lynch proposes greater coordination between those involved in Supreme Court litigation (Lynch 2004, 67–9).

arguments, elaborating in a way the party could not (Pfeffer 1981, 105; Ennis 1984, 605–6). Sometimes the information provided by *amici* comes not from what they argue but from their very presence. Research on the impact of attorney experience has shown that in some cases, parties represented by inexperienced attorneys may benefit from the presence of more experienced attorneys or more well-known groups appearing as *amici* (Pfeffer 1981, 106; Wasby 1984, 114; Simmons 2009, 204). Even without the benefit of greater experience or reputation, the simple presence of a number of groups as *amici* can serve to focus the Court's attention, highlighting specific case salience or broader public opinion (Ivers 1992, 251; Pfeffer 1981, 109; Spriggs and Wahlbeck 1997, 369).

Friend or Foe?

Clearly, there is broad agreement that groups appearing as friends could potentially influence the Court's decision making. Demonstrating that such influence actually does occur, however, is a difficult proposition. The evidence is inconclusive at best and contradictory at worst. Part of the problem comes from the variety of ways scholars have attempted to discern such influence.

Many who have reported positive evidence for the value of *amici* have relied upon anecdotal evidence. Perhaps the most famous example offered is that of *Mapp v. Ohio* (1961) in which the Court's ultimate holding—that the exclusionary rule should apply to the states—was based on a rationale found solely in an *amicus* brief authored by the American Civil Liberties Union (Collins 2004, 815; Day 2001; McGuire and Palmer 1995; Collins 2008, 142). While such seemingly clear-cut examples are hard to find, scholars have noted the influential role of *amici* in *Oregon ex rel. State Land Bd. v. Corvallis Sand and Gravel Co.* (1977), *Webster v. Reproductive Health Services* (1989), *Davis v. Monroe County Board of Education* (1999), and *Teague v. Lane* (1989).[9] Other studies have looked beyond individual cases to trace the impact of *amici* on specific areas of litigation, including church-state relations (Ivers 1992, Pfeffer 1981), gender discrimination (Wolpert 1991), and obscenity law (McGuire 1990).

---

[9] C.f. Kearney and Merrill 2000, 745n5; Collins 2004, 815 citing Behuniak-Long 1991, Kolbert 1989, Sungaila 1999, and Munford 1999.

A few scattered instances of influential *amici* do not prove that on the whole they make a difference. One of the most successful attempt to do so comes from Caldeira and Wright's 1988 study of the certiorari process. Elaborating on the "gatekeeping" research pioneered by Tanenhaus et al. (1963) and further developed by the likes of Ulmer (1983, 1984), Caldeira and Wright developed a multivariate probit model of the influences on the certiorari process for the Court's 1982 term. Their model confirmed previous research that conflict in lower courts increases the likelihood of a case being granted full review, as does the presence of the Solicitor General as petitioner.[10] However, they were also able to demonstrate that the presence of *amicus curiae* briefs at the certiorari stage—either in favor of the Court granting review or not—leads to a similar increase in grant rates (Caldeira and Wright 1988, 1121). While the presence of two or three briefs increases the chance of a case being accepted from approximately .01 to .35 (with all other factors held constant), the same number of briefs in a case with lower court conflict has a .88 chance of being granted (Caldeira and Wright 1988, 1121–2).

A similarly upbeat analysis of *amici* comes from Paul Collins' book *Friends of the Supreme Court* (2008). Drawing upon a dataset of cases decided between 1946 and 2001 and a number of different multinomial models,[11] Collins investigates a number of questions about the nature and impact of *amici*. Two of his empirical findings are particularly relevant. First, the presence of *amicus* briefs does have a discernable impact upon how justices vote—even when controlling for alternative explanatory factors like judicial ideology (Collins 2008, 114, 172). More importantly, briefs appear to have an influence on justices in spite of their ideology. For almost all justices, conservative briefs create con-

---

[10] Much research prior to and after the 1988 article demonstrates the Solicitor General's successful track record before the Court (c.f. Baker 1984; Caplan 1987; Lynch 2004, 46; McGuire 1998; O'Connor 1983; Provine 1980; Puro 1981; Salokar 1992; Scignliano 1971; Segal 1988; Segal and Reedy 1988; Spriggs and Wahlbeck 1997; Ulmer 1984; Ulmer and Willison 1985). Another line of research has begun to trace out the reasons for the SG's impact, as well as that office's role within a system of separated institutions (c.f. Bailey, Kamoie, and Maltzman 2005; Johnson 2003; Meinhold and Shull 1998; Pacelle 2006; Nicholson and Collins 2008).

[11] Collins' data are built off of that gathered by Kearney and Merrill and extended to include 1985 to 2001. For more information, see Kearney and Merrill 2000 and the appendix to Collins 2008.

servative momentum in voting behavior, and the presence of liberal *amici* does the same in a liberal direction (Collins 2004, 114). Collins also finds that increasing numbers of third party briefs increases a justice's propensity to write a concurring or dissenting opinion. By offering the Court additional legal justifications, in effect enriching the information environment, justices have an easier time authoring seriatem opinions because they are effectively handed research and reasoning that they otherwise would have to develop on their own (Collins 2008, 164, 173).

These positive results are matched, though, by studies that are less optimistic about the value of *amici*. One area of uncertainty is the connection between a group's reason for choosing to participate as *amicus* and its eventual impact upon the case—either regarding the actual grant of *certiorari* or the decision on the merits. The traditional view posits a situation of fundamental uncertainty about the Court's decision and suggests that groups become involved to reduce that uncertainty, either by providing information necessary for the decision or by attempting to persuade the Court to rule in line with the groups' own interests. From this perspective, group involvement is a question of choosing appropriate opportunities. At times the choice to participate may not seem like a choice at all, as in situations where groups feel "forced" to participate because of the gravity of the issues involved (Wasby 1984, 113). Alternately, group involvement might occasionally be recruited by attorneys seeking additional support (Baker 1984, 626; Ennis 1984, 603; McGuire 1994, 823).[12]

Several scholars have argued, however, that the arrow of causality runs entirely in the opposite direction. Countering McGuire's findings about attorneys, Hansford has demonstrated that interest groups are actually less likely to submit briefs when the parties in a case are repre-

---

[12] There is, of course, one other special category of group involvement. On a regular basis, the Supreme Court formally requests the Solicitor General to participate in a case as an *amicus*. The nature of such invitations highlights the complex role of the SG: representative of the current administration, but also neutral source of legal counsel. Pacelle argues that when the Solicitor General's briefs are separated into voluntary and invited briefs, one finds a clear distinction. Most notably, in cases where the SG was invited, the resulting arguments show no statistical connection to presidential ideology; the reverse is true for cases where the Solicitor General' involvement is voluntary (Pacelle 2006, 322).

sented by experienced attorneys (Hansford 2004, 226).[13] More importantly, though, several studies have shown that in some situations groups choose to participate as *amici* not because of their ability to affect the outcome, but because they believe from the start that the outcome will be in their interest. This is particularly relevant for membership-based interest groups. Participating in cases with a low risk of failure can lead to the demonstrated track record of success they need in order to secure and grow their membership base (Epstein 1991, 348; Hansford 2004; Kearney and Merrill 2000, 824–5; Collins 2004; Collins 2006). While this selective behavior may not entirely disprove the impact that *amici* can have, it goes a long away towards suggesting that finding such impact will be difficult.

Other research has tried to settle the lingering question of whether the Court is most influenced by the simple presence of *amici* or by some aspect of the briefs themselves. While the difference between the two might appear slight, it is empirically testable. If the former is true, statistical models should point to the number of groups co-filing a brief as a significant independent variable. Several studies, though, have found no such effect (Collins 2004, 822; Caldeira and Wright 1990, 800; Lynch 2004, 59; Collins 2008, 179–80). The standard explanation for this relies upon the insights of signaling theory. For information to serve as a signal to a decision-maker, it must be costly to the sender (Banks and Sobel 1987; Caldeira and Wright 1988, 1112; Crawford and Sobel 1992; Epstein and Knight 1999, 234n23; Farrell and Rabin 1996, 104). Viewed from this perspective, simply joining another group's *amicus* brief costs very little. On the other hand recent estimates of the cost of actually preparing an *amicus* brief place the figure at $50,000—high enough that most groups must pick and choose which cases to participate in (Lynch 2004, 57; Wasby 1984, 115). Looking at cases decided between the 1946 and 2001 terms, Collins has found that once *amici* do decide to join a case, the overall number of briefs becomes important. Controlling for a number of factors, including individual ideology, a justice's propensity to vote conservatively or liberally in a case reflects whether there was a greater number of conservative or liberal *amici* (Collins 2008, 114). The greater the imbalance on one side

---

[13] It should be noted that Hansford's findings do confirm conventional wisdom that groups may be enticed to participate as *amici* when the attorneys in a case are relatively inexperienced (Pfeffer 1981, 106; Simmons 2009, 204; Wasby 1984, 114).

or the other, the more noticeable the impact on the justices' votes (Collins 2006, 19).

Of course, focusing on the simple numerical presence of *amici* really says nothing about how—or even if—an *amicus* brief was actually used by the Court. Collins himself notes that "this analysis is limited in that it cannot definitely tell us the *exact* mechanism under which amicus briefs influence the justices' decision making" (Collins 2008, 177). One solution to this problem, pursued by many, is to scan written opinions and intra-court communication for references to *amici* or to arguments they make in their briefs. In essence this approach takes traditional anecdotal evidence for the influence of *amici* and attempts to render it testable on a large scale. While early research of this kind relied upon human-generated content analysis, more recent work takes advantage of the textual analysis software used to detect plagiarism (c.f. Corley 2008).

The results of such efforts have been mixed. Justices do in fact cite *amicus curiae* briefs at a noticeable rate. Writing about the natural court under Chief Justice Rehnquist from 1994–2003, Owens and Epstein find that in cases involving at least one *amicus*, the opinion of the Court referenced an *amicus* 38% of the time (Owens and Epstein 2005, 130). The authors also note that in some particular issue areas, namely privacy and civil rights, the justices cite *amicus* briefs over 50% of the time (131). Kearney and Merrill performed a similar analysis for the years 1946 through 1995, finding that citation rates have been rising over time, averaging approximately 28% for the entire period (Kearney and Merrill 2000, 758). Other studies have shown that citation rates are roughly similar in majority, concurring and dissenting opinions (Koshansky 1977, 61); that during conferences justices do discuss the preferences of other institutional actors, as revealed in *amicus* briefs (Epstein and Knight 1999, 230); and that the Court seems more likely to cite arguments raised in briefs for the petitioner than for the respondent (Spriggs and Wahlbeck 1997, 373–4).[14] It also appears that justices vary in terms of how freely they borrow material from briefs (Corley 2008).

Frustrating this line of research, however, is the fact that it might seriously underreport the importance of *amici* while at the same time

---

[14] This last point is not without controversy since other studies namely Kearney and Merrill's, have found that *amici* filed for the respondent seem to fair better before the Court (Kearney and Merrill 2000, 749–50).

overstating what can be conclusively decided from a simple reference to a brief. Focusing solely on privacy cases, Samuels has found many instances where the Court clearly made use of information and arguments presented by *amici* but did so without proper attribution (Samuels 2004, xii). If this behavior is wide-spread, relying upon explicit references to *amici* might underreport their true influence. But even if scholars were able to locate all references to *amici*, both explicit and implicit, several questions would remain unanswered. First, why is it that *amici* get cited? While it certainly could be that the Court finds the information and arguments in third party briefs to be helpful, and therefore incorporates them, the Court might also refer to *amici* in some instances simply because there happen to be so many of them. In *Grutter v. Bollinger* (2003), for example, briefs were filed by some 84 groups; including individuals participating as *amici*, the number climbs to more than 100 (Owens and Epstein 2005, 131; Collins 2008, 166).[15] Simple common sense would lead us to believe that Justice O'Connor's majority opinion would have to make some reference to them—as it did.[16]

Even without such a flood of briefs, it seems reasonable to expect references to occur occasionally. That does not prove, though, that the *amici* in question have actually influenced the Court. References may be incidental to the actual legal reasoning and holdings of a case, or may reflect preferences and decisions that would have been made anyway. The situation is no easier if we narrow our focus and examine whether the Court explicitly accepted legal arguments made by *amici*. Many points made by *amici* simply echo those already made by the parties (Johnson 2001, 339; Pfeffer 1981, 105; Shapiro 2008, 17). When the Court adopts such a point, it is impossible to say if the decisive impact was made by the party, the *amicus*, or some combination of the two.

Trying to untangle the connection between *amici* and the parties they represent, research has also focused on identifying the differences between situations where *amici* add new information versus simply

---

[15] *Gratz* and *Grutter*, when combined as they were for oral argument, hold the record for total briefs: the former with 64 and the latter with 40. The record for most *amici* belonging to one docket number goes to the second amendment case of *District of Columbia v. Heller* (2008). See Shapiro 2008 for extensive details on the different *amici* involved.

[16] O'Connor went so far as to cite an *amicus* as she delivered the opinion of the Court—a somewhat more unusual event (Lynch 2004, 33–4).

reiterating existing arguments. Though third party briefs are traditionally thought of as expanding upon the parties, Spriggs and Wahlbeck find evidence to the contrary. In the Court's 1992 term, 67% of all briefs *amicus* offered new arguments with 25.1% composed entirely thereof. However, almost 75% of briefs reiterated existing information and nearly 33% did so exclusively (Spriggs and Wahlbeck 1997, 373). More interesting, though, is the multivariate model the authors created that incorporates the type of information provided while also testing several competing hypotheses about *amici.*[17] In a rather direct contradiction of conventional wisdom, they find that the Court was actually less likely to use a brief's arguments if they exclusively added to the case (Spriggs and Wahlbeck 1997, 374). Briefs that exclusively reiterated arguments were likely to be referred to 63% of the time compared to only 26% for those that exclusively added (Spriggs and Wahlbeck 1997, 379–80). Briefs that combined the two had a 61% chance of being cited. The authors conclude, somewhat hesitantly, that reiterating information does not make a brief more likely to be cited but that exclusively adding information does drastically decrease the chance (Spriggs and Wahlbeck 1997, 381).

Spriggs and Wahlbeck's findings may have been unexpected, but they do make sense in a broader context. In *Friends of the Supreme Court*, Collins hypothesizes that the presence of *amicus* briefs might not only impact the votes that justices make, but may also affect the consistency of their voting patterns. Justices do need information to make decisions and *amici* can offer it (c.f. McAtee and McGuire 2007, 274). But as the number of *amici* increases, the amount of information available can increase beyond levels that are helpful and can contribute to information overload (Collins 2008, 120). The chief result is decisional uncertainty, in which the justices' voting behavior becomes less predictable. Collins tests this hypothesis in a heteroskedastic probit model and finds that that increasing numbers of *amicus* briefs do directly increase the variance in votes (Collins 2008, 131).[18] While these

---

[17] Spriggs and Wahlbeck incorporate tests to examine the impact of *amicus* party status, *amicus* attorney expertise, *amicus* support for petitioners, the size of the *amicus* coalition (cosigners), the ideological direction of the *amicus* brief, and the presence of the Solicitor General (Spriggs and Wahlbeck 1997, 380–1). Only the latter two proved to be statistically significant.

[18] Collins also finds several other factors to impact variance. Cases that are politically salient feature less variance. On the other hand, cases of a solely statutory nature and those with lower court conflict have greater variance. The

findings do call into question the presumption that *amici*, as founts of new information, are a good thing, Collins makes the additional point that judicial scholars need to be cautious about their use of variables that measure *amicus* briefs. Multiple studies use a count of the total number of *amicus* briefs as a proxy for a case's importance. Rather than decreasing variance as a measure of salience would, these measures do the opposite and therefore are poor instruments for measuring a case's salience (Collins 2008, 133).

Despite the clarity of these findings, debate continues about whether *amici* should add or reiterate arguments. To assess the importance of friend briefs, Kelly Lynch conducted a series of interviews with former Supreme Court clerks—relying upon a sample of clerks covering the past forty years as well as the offices of sixteen justices (Lynch 2004, 38). Drawing on the admittedly conflicting comments made by the clerks, Lynch offers potential *amici* the following advice: "to the greatest extent possible, avoid repeating the information presented in the merits brief of the party it supports and in the other amicus briefs. Clerks cited *verbatim iteration* to be the fatal flaw of an amicus brief. A serviceable brief must be additive to the party discussion" (Lynch 2004, 67).[19]

Perhaps the most direct test of the impact of *amici* comes from Songer and Sheehan's comparison of cases with and without *amici*. Extending a method used by Epstein and Rowland (1991), the authors employed "precision matching" to identify pairs of cases that were identical on important aspects, such as year, natural court, issue area, and litigant type—but which varied in the presence or absence of *amici* (Songer and Sheehan 1993, 343). Having thus controlled for most of the factors discussed above, their model should be able to determine

---

author also finds that as a justice stays longer on the Court, their voting variance increases as well—the opposite of what he had hypothesized (Collins 2008, 134–8).

[19] The major weakness of Lynch's account is that she tends to downplay the case against the value of *amici*. After discussing a number of positive accounts about *amici* (many of the ones discussed above), she mentions only two contrasting studies and summarizes rather weakly by saying "while most of the aforementioned studies tend to support the contention that *amicus* briefs do in fact make some difference, they are not conclusive" (Lynch 2004, 37). Her discussion of the literature, though, fails to include the Spriggs and Wahlbeck's article—probably the most rigorous and systematic attempt to test conventional wisdom about *amici*.

whether the presence of *amici* serves to affect case outcomes. While the complexity of finding identically matched cases makes the authors somewhat hesitant, their results are not encouraging. The presence of an *amicus curiae* in support of one party but not the other appears to have no effect on the likelihood of winning the case (Songer and Sheehan 1993, 350). Even when examining cases with a greater number of groups—three briefs on one side versus none on the other—the results were the same.

ORAL ARGUMENTS

Past studies of oral arguments have paralleled those of briefs *amicus curiae*. For example, a fair amount of anecdotal evidence exists about the importance of oral arguments. In his book on the Court, Chief Justice Rehnquist begins a section of advice for potential oral advocates by assuring his readers that "[i]n a significant minority of the cases in which I have heard oral argument, I have left the bench feeling differently about a case than I did when I came on the bench. The change is seldom a full one-hundred-and-eighty-degree swing, and I find that it is most likely to occur in cases involving areas of law with which I am least familiar" (Rehnquist 2002, 243-4). He goes on to note that an "effective" advocate will, in the end, "have something to do with how a case comes out" (244).[20] Similar statements from Justices Jackson, Powell, Hughes, White, and Brennan are also on the record (Johnson 2004, 14-6; Stern, Gressman, et al. 2002, 672).

Scholars and journalists routinely draw upon these accounts or on isolated examples to suggest that predictive power can be found in the questions that justices ask (Benoit 1989; Biskupic 1999; Cohen 1978; Galloway 1989; Lane 2003a, 2003b). For others, the way that justices conduct questioning might be as important as the question itself. Looking at the transcripts for eleven obscenity cases, McFeeley and Ault (1979) suggest that a justice's "toughness" in questioning reveals their intended vote. In a number of works, Schubert et al. have followed a

---

[20] Rehnquist suggests that are two primary functions of oral arguments. The first is the formal and ceremonial opportunity for counsel to engage in a discussion with those who will decide their case. Oral arguments, however, are also an opportunity for justices to announce, however subtly, their uncertainty or confusion about a case and have those concerns addressed by counsel in a way that also communicates the justice's beliefs to his or her colleagues (Rehnquist 2002, 244).

similar approach but have included physical posture, vocal inflection or mannerisms, expletives, and "negative aspect" (Schubert et al. 1990, 1991a, 1991b, 1992). In a set of ten cases, Shullman recorded the wording of the Court's questions, who asked the question, as well as their content and demeanor. She combined these aspects to rate questions on a scale of one, most helpful, to five, most hostile to the attorney and their party (Shullman 2004, 273). Her results suggest that the party that gets most intensively questioned will likely lose the case. Wrightsman examined twenty-four cases, evenly split among salient and non-salient cases, and found that question counts alone do not predict a case's fate but that a broader set of question dynamics might (Wrightsman 2008).

Whether the focus is on the questions or the questioning, all the studies mentioned suffer from two major problems. First, the limited number of cases they consider severely limits their external validity. Second, most of these studies fail to include a solid theoretical grounding. It seems reasonable to believe that some connection exists between what justices do at arguments and how they ultimately vote. But is there a necessary link between these two events? A justice who sounds cynical or overly hostile might simply believe that oral arguments are a time to push counsel to go beyond the limits of their arguments (c.f. Phillips and Carter 2009a, 27). Smith suggests something along these lines when he notes that the justices "probe the attorneys' minds for additional arguments and justifications to make their case opinions more complete and compelling" (1993, 271). The problem with any "performance based" analysis of oral arguments is the assumption that justices have no more sophisticated reason for their behavior than telegraphing their preferences to counsel.

Despite these problems, the attractiveness of intuitive evaluations of oral argument is hard to break, largely because of their apparent predictive power. Linda Greenhouse, a long time Supreme Court reporter, was able to correctly predict the outcomes of more cases in the 2002 term than were teams of political scientists or legal scholars (Greenhouse 2004). A new body of research is trying to correct the two faults common to prior research. Johnson, Black, Goldman, and Treul have taken the logic of question volume analysis and applied it to a large-N study of all argued cases between 1979 and 1995.[21] While their work

---

[21] The Supreme Court's 1979 term currently represents a barrier before which analysis of oral arguments is difficult because of the availability of argument transcripts.

does not currently include any aspects of the questioning, they do confirm that the side most questioned appears more likely to lose its case (Johnson et al 2009, 20). This finding holds even when their model focuses on the number of words spoken by the justices instead of the number of questions. Subsequent research has expanded and solidified their earlier findings (c.f. Johnson, Black, and Wedeking 2008; Johnson, Black, and Wedeking 2009; Johnson, Black, Treul 2009). Other scholars have also begun expanding on this work to tease apart how justices vary in their questioning behavior and how the purpose of justices' questions impacts case outcomes (c.f. Epstein, Landes, and Posner 2009; Phillips and Carter 2009a, 2009b, 2009c, 2009d).

Another more developed line of research focuses less explicitly on the questions and instead considers oral arguments as one of many potential sources of information for the justices. This approach has shown successfully that justices use oral arguments to: raise new questions of policy, explore the choices available to them, and gauge the response of other actors to said policies (Johnson 2001, 340); explore new issues rather than those previously mentioned in briefs (Johnson 2001, 342); consider previously unraised questions of applicable precedent or threshold issues (Johnson 2001, 343); and evaluate the preferences of other political actors, namely the legislative and executive branches (Johnson 2004, 128). In addition, during their conferences the justices refer to issues raised at oral arguments (Johnson 2004, 77–80); mention them in intra-Court memoranda (Johnson 2004, 90–1); and ultimately incorporate them into final opinions (Johnson 2004, 119–21).

Johnson, along with Wahlbeck and Spriggs, have also conducted research that examines oral arguments based on the performance of the attorneys involved. Drawing upon Justice Blackmun's graded evaluations of attorney quality, they have found that justices systematically vote in favor of "higher quality oral advocates" (Johnson, Wahlbeck, and Spriggs 2006, 111). As with Collins' analysis of *amicus* briefs, this effect holds for justices of all ideological perspectives. Blackmun's notes, while essentially a subjective evaluation, appear to be strongly related to more objective measures of attorney experience such as law school background and previous Supreme Court oral advocacy (Johnson, Wahlbeck, and Spriggs 2006, 107–8). They also appear to be unrelated to Blackmun's own personal ideology, making them a reasonable proxy for a broad set of potential measures of attorney quality. Johnson, Spriggs, and Wahlbeck 2007 reiterates this finding and goes so far as to suggest that inexperienced counsel should seek out expert advocates to present their case to the Court (61).[22]

CONNECTING THE DOTS

The literature paints an extremely mixed picture about *amici curiae*. Tradition believes in their value, but actual empirical studies have at various times supported, refuted, and contradicted that wisdom. In this book, I will add to the discussion by examining an aspect of *amicus* involvement that has not received any systematic investigation: the presence of *amici* at oral argument.[23] Between 1953 and 1985, in an average of 8 percent of cases each term, at least one *amicus* shared time at oral argument with the attorneys for the parties. While this number is low compared to the overall number of *amici* in cases, the fact that such oral *amici* exist at all is interesting.

The reasons for the disparity in numbers can be partially traced to the Court's procedures. Supreme Court Rule 37 requires that those hoping to submit an *amicus* brief secure the written consent of all the parties. Lacking such consent, the potential *amicus* can petition the Court for leave to file. As described above, the Court has seemed unwilling to use this power to restrict the presence of *amici* and lighten its workload. Over the thirteen years that they studied, O'Connor and Epstein found that only eight percent of petitions were denied (1983, 41).[24] A different story emerges for groups hoping to appear at oral arguments. In addition to Rule 37, such *amici* must satisfy the requirements in Rule 28. Two aspects of this rule are noteworthy. First is the requirement that the *amicus* must once again secure the permission of the party on whose side they would argue. And since the Court rarely increases the

[22] Johnson, Spriggs, and Wahlbeck 2007 does more than simply repeat the findings of the 2006 piece. Perhaps the more important contribution, still based on Blackmun's notes, is that justices can use their time at oral arguments to gauge their colleagues presumed positions on the case in support of an effort to predict and build potential coalitions for the vote on the merits (62). See also Johnson, Black, and Wedeking 2009; Johnson, Black, and Wedeking 2010; Wedeking 2010.

[23] For a good example of how research about oral argument proceeds without even noticing the presence of oral *amici*, see Epstein, Landes, and Posner 2009.

[24] To reach this number they excluded petitions that were denied for being untimely or that were submitted by the prolific attorney Alan Ernest on behalf of Pro-Life groups. Adding in these motions, however, only brings the Court's total denials to eleven percent (O'Connor and Epstein 1983, 41).

length of arguments, such parties must be willing to divide their own time. Second, the Court seems to actively discourage the presence of *amici* at argument by making explicit that, absent the party's consent, they will grant a petition for leave to participate in oral arguments "only in the most extraordinary circumstances" (Stern, Gressman, et al. 2002, 684; see also Lazarus 2008).

Whatever the underlying reason—a desire to keep arguments streamlined or a belief that third parties provide no extra value by appearing at arguments—*amicus* argumentation is in fact rare. It is because of this scarcity that I believe their presence at oral arguments might help clarify what impact *amici* do have on the Court's cases.

In chapter two I examine oral *amici* as a phenomenon that itself needs explanation. Drawing on the vast literature that emphasizes the information needs of the Court (c.f. Caldeira and Wright 1990; Epstein and Knight 1999; Hansford 2004; Johnson 2004; Lazarus 2008), I conceptualize third parties as one potential solution.[25] In particular, I examine the following:

> ***Information Provision Hypothesis.*** Third party friends of the court will be more likely to appear at oral arguments in cases characterized by an information deficit.

Two general aspects of a Supreme Court case seem relevant for identifying the presence of an information deficit. The first is the case's "demographics:" the traits of a case's background and history that either limit or compound the number of decisional elements that justices must consider. A case that features dissent among lower circuit courts of appeals, for example, could be considered more complex than a case without such dissent. Resolving that complexity requires an increased need for information. Appearing at oral argument allows an *amicus* to provide an even greater amount of information to the justices than they can by merely filing a brief.

The second case aspect which points toward information deficits comes from the performative nature of Supreme Court cases. Johnson,

[25] The research described above does outline one major challenge to the importance of increasing the Court's information. Collins 2004 hypothesizes and finds that too much information, in the form of *amicus* briefs, may lead to greater unpredictability in the justices votes due to information overload. While I recognize the importance of this wrinkle in my overall theory, I leave a proper treatment of the issue for a later work.

Spriggs, and Wahlbeck have found that the quality of an attorney contributes to whether the Court will vote in that attorney's favor (2006, 2007; see also Lazarus 2008, 1549; Corley 2008). This echoes a number of studies that have found that attorneys themselves matter (c.f. McGuire 1995; McGuire and Caldeira 1993; Kearney and Merrill 2000; Martinek 2006). If oral arguments are an opportunity for the Court to gather information on its own (Johnson 2004), it stands to reason that attorneys, particular their skill or lack thereof, can serve as a mediating force on the justices' information gathering. An unprepared, unknowledgeable advocate may frustrate the argument process. On the other hand, the justices may be increasingly receptive to "those who have shown themselves capable of reducing [their] informational burdens" (McGuire 1998, 509). Accordingly, in chapter two I examine how various measures of attorney experience might tie into the Court's information needs and when oral *amici* are likely to appear. I follow this analysis with a narrative description of three cases, focusing on how the oral *amicus* in each case shaped the case overall.

Chapter three deals with the perennial question of finding the impact of *amici*. Using Gibson's *United States Supreme Court Database, Phase II: 1953–1985* (1997), I develop a set of models to test the following:

> ***Amicus Impact Hypothesis.*** The presence of *amici* at oral argument will lead to an increased likelihood of decisions being made in the *amicus*' favor.

Gibson's inclusion of data on *amicus* participation over a broad time span will allow me to control for other influences on the resolution of cases. With minor modifications, the same data will allow me to test this hypothesis at both the case level (whether oral amici influence the disposition of cases) and at the level of individual justices' votes. I anticipate that aggregate-level effects of amici will be significant but modest. At the justice level, I expect my results to parallel the findings in Collins 2008: justices will be swayed by oral *amici* regardless of their own ideology, but justices who are ideologically moderate may see a greater influence.

As I attempted to make clear in my discussion of the literature, observing a statistically significant impact from the mere presence of *amici* does not fully explain the mechanism behind or the importance of that impact. To that end, chapter three concludes with an attempt to measure if the arguments provided by *amici* during oral argument find their way into the Court's majority opinion. I rely upon the technique from Johnson 2004 that involves identifying the specific holdings in the syllabus of the Court's opinion and coding for whether a matching reference can be found in the case's written briefs and in the questions asked by the justices. Using this method will have two immediate practical consequences. First, I will be able to compare my results with Johnson's to determine if the Court's information usage varies between cases with and without oral *amici*. Second, by tracking the Court's holdings to as any many sources as possible, I will be able to weigh-in on the strategic question of whether *amici* succeed most when they focus on reiterating the parties' information or when they add new information to a case.

Chapter four reviews the book's empirical results and assesses their implications for future research. Given that this is the first round of research on the subject, the results will be an important indication of whether oral *amici* deserve future attention. Though only two have been mentioned so far, this project is situated at the intersection of three separate literatures—those on *amici*, oral arguments, and attorney experience. Consequently, a variety of future projects readily suggest themselves. Should my findings prove significant, they also have the potential to inform the development of those literatures themselves. Johnson et al 2009, for example, posits that the outcome of a case is related to the behavior of the justices during argument. A more complete picture of oral argument, however, should include attorneys as part of the equation. This would involve both the level of experience and skill that counsel bring to the case, but also the way in which the immediate reactions of counsel to the justices' questioning influences the course of argument itself.

Chapter four concludes by situating my findings within a broader context. For decades, scholars and amateur Court-watchers have been fascinated by the idea of the "swing voter"—a justice who, by virtue of her ideological relationship with the other justices, serves as the final deciding vote for a majority coalition. The concept of the swing voter stretches back at least as far as Justice Owen Roberts' vote in *West Coast Hotel Co. v. Parrish* (300 U.S. 379, 1937). In addition to being the crucial vote for the case's outcome, Roberts' switch is seen as breaking the logjam of New Deal legislation. His vote changed not only the disposition of a single case but ushered in a whole new era of Supreme Court jurisprudence.

While few justices are as pivotal as Roberts was, swing voters are a reality. When a Court is closely divided and one justice holds such influence, it is only natural that extra attention should be paid to how and why the swing vote arrives at her decisions. For Supreme Court practitioners, part of arguing a case turns into developing "a plan likely…to win the favor of" the Court's current swing voter (Munter 2008, 695). Old decisions are analyzed and public statements parsed to discern where the swing stands and what types of arguments will appeal to her.

The results of this research have the potential to inform these strategic decisions. Targeting particular justices presumes that the swing is like a hidden treasure—an ideological position or favorite legal frame waiting to be unearthed. This static account is at odds with the perspective I establish in the following chapters. While the justices' ideologies are a significant factor in their decision making, not everything about a case can be easily predicted in advance. The presence of *amici curiae* at oral argument represents one type of wild card. I argue that the reasons why friends appear at argument have less to do with the justices' ideologies and more to do with objective information needs. More importantly, I believe that oral *amici* have the potential to shape the justices' votes, potentially altering the outcome of a case independent of the justices' own policy preferences. This becomes increasingly important in situations when the Court is closely divided and the so-called swing voter holds the balance of power. The final outcome of such cases might not depend on the attorneys' ability to pinpoint the swing's position but rather in how that justice reacts to the unusual presence of oral *amici*.

CHAPTER 2

Amici: Who and When

Most readers are likely familiar with the 2003 affirmative action cases *Grutter v. Bollinger* and *Gratz v. Bollinger*, as well as the 2008 case of *District of Columbia v. Heller*, which dealt with the second amendment's potential protections of firearm ownership. For the moment, these cases represent the high water mark in *amicus* participation. Depending on how one counts, *Gratz* and *Grutter* combined saw the filing of over 100 briefs (Owens and Epstein 2005, 131; Collins 2008, 166). *Heller* holds the record for a single docket number, at 68 (Shapiro 2008, 15).

Less well known, perhaps, is the case of Puyallup Tribe v. Department of Game of Washington Et Al. (391 U.S. 392, 1968). Unlike the broadly divisive issues at the heart of Grutter, Puyallup concerned the ongoing controversy between the State of Washington and the Puyallup Indian tribe regarding fishing rights in the state's rivers. In particular, the tribe alleged that rights guaranteed them under the 1854 Treaty of Medicine Creek protected their right to fish using set nets, despite the fact that doing so was illegal under Washington law. The Supreme Court disagreed, interpreting the treaty as protecting the right to fish but not the right to fish in whatsoever manner the tribe might desire. In his opinion for a unanimous court, Justice Douglas argued that "the manner of fishing, the size of the take, the restriction of commercial fishing, and the like may be regulated by the State in the interest of conservation, provided the regulation meets appropriate standards and does not discriminate against the Indians." (391 U.S. 392, 395, 398).[26]

For the years between 1953 and 1986, *Puyallup* holds the honor of being the case with the highest *amicus* participation at oral argument.[27] That number, however, is far lower than *Grutter's* record. An assistant to the Solicitor General and two Assistant Attorneys General—for the states of Idaho and Oregon—together made for three additional attorneys sharing argument time with the litigants.[28]

This gross disparity between the maximum number of *amicus* brief filers and oral *amici* demonstrates the differential nature of third party participation before the Court. While the maximum number of briefs is high, over the past half century the number of cases with at least one

---

[26] The 1968 case did not completely settle the dispute between the Puyallup and the State of Washington. The parties returned to the Supreme Court in again in 1973 (*Department of Game of Washington v. Puyallup Tribe Et Al.*, 414 U.S. 44). This *Puyallup II*, with Douglas again writing for a unanimous court, ruled against the State and found that the Department of Game's regulations unfairly limited Tribe fishing in favor of sportfishing. Then finally, in 1977, the Court heard *Puyallup III* (*Puyallup Tribe, Inc., Et Al. v. Department of Game of Washington Et Al.*, 433 U.S. 165). Perhaps fitting for the long-running saga, the majority opinion was authored by John Paul Stevens, who took Douglas' seat on the Court. With Brennan and Marshall in dissent, the Court seemed both tired of the ongoing controversy and eager to spread wins and losses among all the parties. Stevens' opinion reiterated that tribal sovereign immunity generally protected the tribe from action in state courts. A claim to unlimitable fishing rights on the reservation, as the tribe was claiming, would frustrate the state's efforts to balance tribal and sportfishing needs. Ultimately, the Court upheld the Washington courts' attempt to establish fair fishing limits for the Puyallup but protected the tribe from having to surrender individual members' fishing records to state officials.

[27] To be technically correct, *Puyallup* holds this honor only if one puts to the side *Brown v. Board of Education* (349 U.S. 294, 1955). From several points-of-view, *Brown* is an outlier. This is certainly true regarding oral *amici*. The case featured seven additional oral advocates: 1) Solicitor General Sobeloff, participating at the Court's invitation; 2) Thomas J. Gentry, Attorney General of Arkansas; 3) Richard W. Ervin, Attorney General of Florida; 4) C. Ferdinand Sybert, Attorney General of Maryland; 5) I. Beverly Lake, Assistant Attorney General of North Carolina; 6) Mac Q. Williamson, Attorney General of Oklahoma; and 7) John Ben Shepperd, Attorney General of Texas.

[28] John S. Martin, Jr., counsel for the United States, later served as a United States Attorney in Manhattan from 1980 to 1983 and was later appointed by George H.W. Bush to the U.S. District Court for the Southern District of New York. He served on the court for thirteen years.

amicus brief has also skyrocketed. At the beginning of Warren Burger's tenure as Chief Justice, less than forty percent of cases featured *amici*; this number had almost doubled by the end of his time on the Court (Owens and Epstein 2005, 128; Lazarus 2008, 1513; Simmons 2009, 190). The Rehnquist court's 2001 term featured a rate of almost 95 percent *amicus* participation (Owens and Epstein 2005: 128). While the timespans are not identical, between 1953 and 1985 the percentage of cases per term with at least one oral *amicus* never rose above 15.67 percent (in 1963), and averaged 8.01 percent per term over the period, with a standard deviation of 4.04 (see Figure 2.1). While these numbers certainly feature an upward trend like that of briefs, oral *amici* are still much less common.

Figure 2.1: Percentage of cases with at least one oral *amicus*, displayed by term

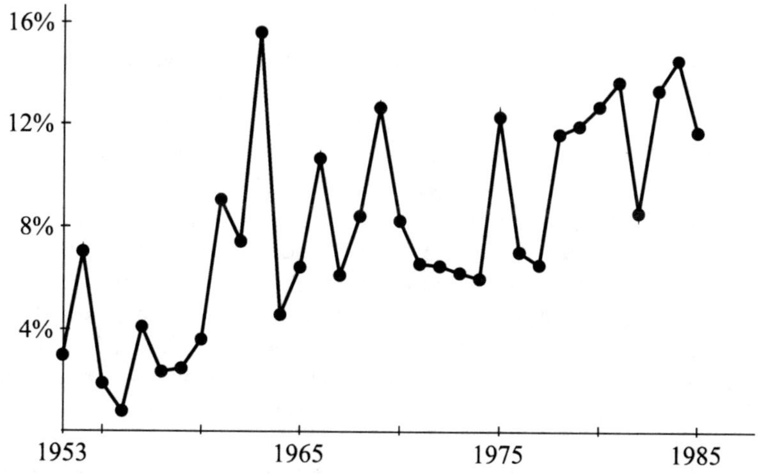

[†] Gibson 1997, *United States Supreme Court judicial database: Phase II.*

Several questions can be asked about oral *amici*. Why does the Court continue to allow the practice? Do oral *amici* make any difference in the outcome of a case, either in disposition or in legal holdings? The goal of this chapter is to answer a more general question: when are *amici* likely to appear at oral arguments?[29] The literature available suggests two different categories of factors could explain a third party's presence at argument. One explanation could be the "objective" factors of the cases themselves. *Amici* may be more likely to be allowed into oral argument in cases that are demonstrably different from others, perhaps in content or complexity. A second explanation is that *amici* might participate not because of the case but because of the counsel representing the parties. Since research does show that the quality and experience of counsel has an impact upon court proceedings,[30] the presence of *amici* could be a function of some aspect of the attorneys themselves, such as experience or the lack thereof. After reviewing prior findings in both of these areas, I will present the results of an exploratory analysis of the importance of personnel factors on the presence of oral *amici.*

CASE DEMOGRAPHICS

The question of when to expect to find oral *amici* is analogous to the slightly broader question of when *amici* should be found in a case at all. A general perception of the influence of *amici*, combined with the Court's current permissiveness in granting motions for leave to file as *amicus*, make cases without third parties the exception.[31] As outlined in the first chapter oral arguments place much greater demands on the justices and the parties than does simply filing a brief. Time, in particular, is scarce. It is rarely extended beyond the allotted hour. To benefit from an accompanying *amicus* at argument means a party must reduce its own counsel's time before the justices. For a number of reasons, there are strong incentives against having *amici* at oral argument. Nonetheless, general findings about the participation of *amici* may still be relevant.

Amici get involved in a case through one of three avenues. First, the Court itself might extend an invitation to join in a case. Such a privilege is generally only extended to the Solicitor General of the

---

[29] Note that this is a question of fact and not desire or volition. This is not the same as asking why *amici* would want to participate at oral arguments, why the parties would want them to participate, or why the justices would allow them to be present. Each of these is an interesting question, but is not the goal of this chapter.

[30] C.f. McGuire 1993, McGuire 1995, Johnson et al. 2006.

[31] C.f. O'Connor and Epstein 1983, 41.

United States—and is treated as more of a summons than an invitation (Nicholson and Collins 2007, 4). Pacelle has found that when participating as an invited *amicus*, compared to when the Office chooses to participate voluntarily, the Solicitor General appears to function as a "fifth clerk" for the justices, helping provide neutral information (Pacelle 2006, 322). Pacelle's finding broadens the common perspective that the SG as a "tenth justice," promoting the position of the administration as a tempering influence for the Court's potential decisions. While the SG can certainly fill that function, Pacelle notes that it only does so when its involvement comes from its own volition and not the Court's. These findings remain in tension with earlier work on invitations extended to the Solicitor General, such as Johnson 2003. Using a rare events analysis to look at cases in Gibson's 1997 data which include invitations, Johnson found that the Court calls for the SG's views when the administration has a noticeable amount of political capital (444). In such circumstances, it is more likely that the administration could sanction a Court that strays too far from the President's preferred outcomes. Inviting the Solicitor General is one way the Court can make sanction less likely. Pacelle's article writes off Johnson via a footnote, claiming that the latter used only a subset of cases. The two authors' results, while confusing, might not be entirely contradictory. It seems conceptually possible that the Court's goal in inviting the SG might not be matched by what the office provides. Certainly, the two cannot be entirely reconciled without further study.

Second, *amici* could become involved in a case by being "recruited" by the parties. The Court's formal rules require potential *amici* to detail the extent of their connections with the parties to the case (Kearney and Merrill 2000, 766). The goal of such rules is to prevent parties from outright authorship or financial sponsorship of *amicus* briefs. Little systematic evidence exists, though, about what happens beyond these clear boundaries. It is reasonable to imagine that basic recruitment of third party involvement could still occur without attracting the attention of the Court—or judicial scholars. Drawing on a survey of attorneys involved in Supreme Court litigation, one of the few studies to test for the extent of recruitment found limited results. At least at the certiorari stage, attorneys do recruit *amici* but not regularly (McGuire 1994). Such participation is most likely to be solicited by experienced attorneys who understand the value of a cert-stage *amici*, or to be found in cases with the potential to affect a broad and substantial range of interests (McGuire 1994, 833–4).

The vast majority of *amici*, it would seem, come to the Court of their own volition.[32] The answers to why they choose to do so are probably as varied as the number of *amici* themselves. Wasby's study of the ACLU, NAACP, and the NAACP Legal Defense and Educational Fund (LDF) demonstrates how *amicus* activity reflects specific decisions about an interest group's overall strategy for litigation and social change (Wasby 1984). In his study, Wasby does find some evidence that groups coordinate the initiation of litigation by referring cases to each other or by deferring to better suited groups (101). The decision to enter as an *amicus*, though, is much less other-regarding. Balancing the need to pursue their own goals while limiting their participation so as not to tire the Court of their presence, Wasby notes three reasons that groups often become *amici* (Wasby 1984, 114). The first is to reinforce existing arguments made by the parties or other *amici* (the so-called "me too" function). Second, some groups might participate because they want to reframe the issues to better reflect the group's interests or goals. Third, potential *amici* might be motivated to supplement the parties. This can take the form either of supplementing counsel, compensating for weak or inexperienced attorneys inferior counsel by way of the group's repeat player status. *Amici* might also supplement the litigants' arguments, raising a point that the parties could not or did not address.[33] Groups frequently choose this route when they believe they can make a special contribution to a case, either through their credibility or the quality of the arguments they offer (Wasby 1984, 114–5; see also Epstein 1993, 660). In addition to these three reasons, other scholars have noted that organized interest groups often use litigation, and in particular *amicus* involvement, as a way to promote the group to its current and future members (Epstein 1993, 675–6; Kearney and Merrill 2000, 824–5).

While the motivation for any given *amicus* might be impossible to gauge without a great deal of background knowledge, the function of

---

[32] One might also suggest that some *amici* participate because of an "arms race" phenomena. Lacking any actual contribution to make any eschewing any belief that their brief might be persuasive, Group A might participate in a case because potential rival Group B may choose to do so on the opposing side, and Group A hopes to avoid giving the impression to its members that it has been lax in protecting its interests (Kearney and Merrill 2000, 821; see also Simmons 2009, 205).

[33] For example, *amici* often find it safer to argue for overruling Court precedent than do the parties (Baker 1984, 626).

amici overall can be summarized fairly succinctly. Friends of the court, whether organized interest groups or some other entity, seek to shape the policies generated by the Court's decisions on the merits and the legal rules that it establishes (Hansford 2004, 220).[34] To describe this goal as "policy influence" is to say little about the nature of the *amicus*' motivations. The definition holds equally well for those who seek to be an "impartial friend of the court," as the *amicus curiae* was initially conceived, and for those who reflect Krislov's contention that *amici* in modern American law represent "active participant[s] in the interest group struggle" (Krislov 1963, 703).

Scholars have argued for some time that *amici* seek to shape policy by providing the Court with information (Barker 1967, 54; Barrett and Morris 1993, 210; Caldeira and Wright 1990, 800; Epstein and Knight 1999, 215; Hansford 2004, 220; Wasby et al. 1976, 419). For our purposes, why the Court needs information—that is, the question of how the Court goes about making its decisions—is irrelevant. Whether justices' seek to maximize their own policy preferences, provide a faithful interpretation of current law, preserve the Court's institutional legitimacy, or moderate their views in light of institutional constraints, the justices require information about the circumstances of the case and the consequences of potential decisions (Berman 1966, 77; Caldeira and Wright 1988, 1123; Epstein and Knight 1999, 219; Johnson 2001, 333; Lynch 2004, 40; Segal and Spaeth 2002, 324; Spriggs and Wahlbeck 1997, 367). This "information problem" can be met in several ways. Litigant briefs contain voluminous amounts of information about the background of a case and potential ways to decide it (Johnson 2004, 12). Justices can also rely upon their own research, gathering information from the media, scholarly sources, as well as the case's record from lower courts (Epstein and Knight 1998, 145; Epstein and Knight 1999, 220; Johnson 2004, 12).

If *amici* play a role in meeting the Court's informational needs, it would be logical to find them in what could be called "relatively information-poor setting[s]" (Hansford 2004, 221). Hansford tests this hypothesis, among others, by developing a set of logit models that identify when organized interest groups are likely to file *amicus* briefs in Supreme Court cases. In addition to finding that traditional indicators of a case's "importance" do seem to trigger the presence of *amici*,

---

[34] For more on the issue of whether judges and courts make policy, see Epstein and Knight 1998, 183 and Segal and Spaeth 2002, 6ff.

Hansford finds confirmation for claims that membership-based groups shape their decisions based upon appealing to members (Epstein 1993; Kearney and Merrill 2000).

While very valuable, *amicus* briefs are in fact a two-edged sword. By easily bringing to the Court a wide variety of information, *amici* are often the most cost-effective way—in terms of the justices' own time and resources—for the Court to learn what it needs to (Caldeira and Wright 1988, 1121–2). The problem is that just like litigant briefs, they represent a potentially biased source of information, offered with a particular outcome in mind. It is for this reason that Johnson emphasizes the value of oral arguments. Arguments are the Court's only real opportunity to elicit the information it deems necessary and to subject potential bias to intense scrutiny (Johnson 2004). For the very same reasons that information-poor cases may attract *amici*, their oral counterparts may be likely to appear as well and may in fact prove even more useful to the justices. To that extent, oral *amici* are quite analogous to the presence of *amici* at the cert stage (c.f. Caldeira and Wright 1990, 800).

Not all conceptions of "important" cases, however, are tied to low information conditions. Various research shows that in certain cases, the justices are more likely to rely upon their own preformed policy preferences (Bailey and Maltzman 2005; Nicholson and Collins 2007, 19; Spaeth and Segal 1999, 309–11; Unah and Hancock 2006). Cases that have high political visibility or touch on "hot" political issues, then, should actually be less likely to have oral *amici*.

PERSONNEL FACTORS

A case that has made its way to argument before the Court is a complex entity—an amalgamation of the facts of the case, the legal arguments that have been put forward to justify a particular outcome, as well as the individual attorneys who are prosecuting the case. Within this blend, the attorneys play a uniquely important role. It is their effort and skill which gives the case its final shape. Especially at the appellate stage, attorneys represent independent sources of experience which might raise or lower a litigant's chances of success. And unlike the litigants they may represent, many appellate attorneys are "repeat players" before the Supreme Court.

Concern about the impact of attorney experience and quality is longstanding. Kevin McGuire, both in solo and co-authored articles, has traced the impact of experience. In the area of obscenity law, he found that professional obscenity litigators have a discernable impact upon the Court's case selection, though their impact is less than that made by briefs *amicus curiae* (McGuire and Caldeira 1993, 724). A 1994 article on the connection between *amicus curiae* and attorneys identifies petitioning experience as one of only a few factors that seem to determine if counsel actively recruit *amicus* involvement at the certiorari stage (McGuire 1994, 831). Controlling for other potential factors, McGuire also found that a petitioner with a more experienced attorney increases their estimated chance of winning a case from .66 to .73 (McGuire 1995, 194). Purposefully replicating McGuire's methodology, Kearney and Merrill found that a similar advantage might accrue to petitioners who are supported by *amici* filed by more experienced attorneys (Kearney and Merrill 2000, 814). Examining the U.S. Courts of Appeals, which are admittedly a different venue in many ways, Martinek has established that a lack of attorney experience may serve to deter *amici* from becoming involved because such cases "are less desirable policy-making vehicles" (Martinek 2006, 817).

Lest one believe that the evidence in favor of attorney experience is entirely positive and conclusive, Hansford has found evidence that contradicts McGuire. Conducting a broad study of *amici* that tried to identify the circumstances under which groups are likely to file briefs, Hansford determined that attorneys of above average quality do not appear to have an influence in "soliciting" *amicus* involvement. In fact, an experienced attorney in a case may have a depressive effect on the presence of outside groups (Hansford 2004, 226).

Given the wealth of choices and actions that attorneys must take in pursuing a case, one should expect to find that attorney experience is not universally important. Nonetheless, a more general case for the importance of attorney experience is easy to make. *Amici* are not the only potential solution to the justices' information needs; though they come to the Court on behalf of a specific party, attorneys have the potential to serve the Court as well. So-called "good lawyering" can clarify the legal dimensions of a case and bypass issues of marginal importance, at the same time downplaying personal grand-standing in favor of honest and sober appraisals of the law (McGuire 1995, 189; Lazarus 2008, 1549). An attorney's desire to emulate this model should only increase with the frequency of their appearances before the Court (McGuire 1998, 509). Rather than simply focus on winning one case, an attorney is wise to think about "mak[ing] a positive and memorable impression" which will predispose the Court to think favorably of the attorney in the future (Shapiro 1984, 532). By providing quality "credible advocacy" an attorney hopes that "like many government decisionmakers, the justices should give greater weight to the information supplied by those who have shown themselves capable of reducing [their] informational burdens" (McGuire 1998, 509; McGuire and Caldeira 1993, 719). As one former Assistant to the Solicitor General notes, "what the Court cares about is an attorney's ability to present the case effectively and to respond directly to questions from the Court" (Brinkmann 2003, 69).

While all this is true for attorneys filing briefs with the Court, it is even more true for attorneys in their oral arguments. Briefs benefit from the collaboration of co-authors, and the list of those who also appear "on the brief" says very little about the actual distribution of the workload in the case. An attorney who stands before the Court for argument, though, stands on her own two feet alone. Preparation for the appearance may have been an elaborate affair involving dozens but the argument itself quite directly measures the arguing attorney's own skill and experience (c.f. Brinkmann 2003). The experience is trying enough that at least two attorneys in Supreme Court history have fainted in the Court chamber during argument (Roberts 2005, 73).[35]

As it turns out, this is experience that is generally in short supply. Over the six terms he studied for his 1995 article, McGuire found that only 709 of 3915 attorneys appeared in more than one case (McGuire 1995, 190). Most individuals admitted to the Supreme Court bar never brief or argue more than a single case (McGuire and Caldeira 1993, 719). This is born out by my findings from the 1979 term. Of the more than 200 attorneys that orally argued cases throughout the term, the median number of lifetime cases argued is 1.[36]

That attorney experience is in short supply is made all the more important because of evidence that the justices do pay attention to the

[35] Given that the two attorneys in question were father and son, some allowance should probably be made for family medical history.

[36] The mean lifetime cases argued is much higher—roughly 5.9 cases. The large difference between the two figures can be explained by the fact that a few long-serving members of the Department of Justice had litigation records significantly more extensive than the median attorney. Lawrence G. Wallace, Deputy Solicitor General, holds the record at 157 cases argued. In fact, if one were to aggregate the number of cases argued by all the attorneys who argued in 1979, the fourteen most productive attorneys would account for 51% of all cases.

skill of counsel before them. Research has recently started, for example, on the notes kept by Justice Blackmun during oral arguments—including his comparative rankings and substantive comments about the skill of the counsel before the Court (Johnson et al. 2007, 7). While these argument "grades" represent the subjective opinion of one justice, they correlate strongly with commonly held predictors of attorney quality, such as argument experience (Johnson et al. 2006, 107). Including Blackmun's grades in regression models of the justices' votes also shows that members of the Court have an increased likelihood of taking the side advocated by better counsel, even after controlling for judicial ideology (Johnson et al. 2006, 112).[37]

Inexperienced or "inferior" counsel need not spell the end for a litigant. In part, outside interests base their decision to join a case as *amicus curiae* on estimates of the quality of litigants' counsel (Wasby 1984, 115). A case that appears to be sufficiently important from an outside perspective might elicit the involvement of prestigious or "heavy-weight" groups who would like to lend their reputation in support of weak counsel. Indirect evidence for the usefulness of such "supplemental resources" comes from interviews with Supreme Court law clerks who suggest that *amicus* briefs can prove very valuable in cases with "bad lawyering" (Lynch 2004, 41–2; Budziak 2010, 6).

If *amicus* briefs can play a role in compensating for attorneys with limited experience, it stands to reason that *amici* present during oral arguments could provide even better support—especially if attorneys for *amici* may themselves have greater experience before the bench.[38] It

---

[37] Recent research by Budziak and Lempert call into question some uses of Blackmun's scores, arguing that the grades in part measure the quality of the case itself—not just the attorney (2010). This line of research, however, is still young.

[38] This does appear to be the case. Using the natural log measure of prior arguments that is explained below, the average prior argument experience for regular counsel attorneys is .802, while that for counsel presenting oral argument as *amici* is 2.396. If one examines the same measure looking at the attorneys on each side alone, you find that attorneys for the first party have a value of .948, compared to .656 for the second party—suggesting that in general, attorneys for respondents and appellees are less experienced than their counterparts at the other table. However, attorneys arguing as *amici* for the first party have a mean experience of 2.030, while those arguing for the second party have a mean experience of 2.596—somewhat higher. Looking within cases where *amici* presented argument, the mean difference in experience between *amici* as counsel and their corresponding party was 2.332. For the first party alone, the aver-

stands to reason, then, that the presence of oral *amici* could be triggered by low levels of experience across the board—serving to augment party's counsel.[39] From this I derive the following:

> ***Collective Experience Hypothesis*** **($H_{2.1}$).** A*mici curiae* will be more likely to be found at oral arguments in cases where counsel for both parties are relatively inexperienced.

DATA AND METHODS

Judicial scholars have at their disposal a number of excellent data sets. Unfortunately, the questions addressed by this paper call for data beyond the scope of these standard sources. While Gibson's *United States Supreme Court Judicial Database: Phase II* (1997) is a good starting place for *amicus* research given its inclusion of a large number of *amicus* variables, neither it nor Spaeth's database include details about the attorneys serving as counsel in a given case.

To test the hypotheses in this chapter I began gathering information about all the attorneys who argued a case in the October 1979 term, identifying in Spaeth's database all cases orally argued during that term—a total of 146 docket numbers.[40] I then went back to the original orders for each docket number, which allowed me to gather several pieces of data about each case which are not ordinarily available in Court databases, including the number of orders in each case, the reason for each given order, and the number of requests for *amicus*

---

age difference was 2.030 compared with 2.496 for the second party. Whatever the explanation, it seems clear that counsel for *amici* are more experienced than regular counsel, both across the board and in the cases where they appear.

[39] Another hypothesis that deserves to be investigated is whether oral *amici* are more likely to appear in a case where the counsel for one party is significantly more experienced than counsel for the other party. To properly test that hypothesis, though, will require more data points than a single term offers—and thus must remain a future project.

[40] The 1979 term contains a total of 147 docket numbers. One case, however, seems to warrant exclusion: docket 78–60, *Confederated Tribes of the Colville Indian Reservation et al. v. Washington.* This case was consolidated with 78–630, *Washington et al. v. Confederated Tribes of the Colville Indian Reservation et al.* and decided in that case's opinion (447 U.S. 134). However, the headnotes of the decision indicate that 78–60 was never actually argued. While it might seem reasonable to include this case in analyses that look at case outcomes, it cannot be used for any research that depends upon the argument of the case itself.

participation that were both granted *and* denied. A total of 356 orders were issued for cases in the 1979 term. On average, each docket number had 2.44 orders. Four total docket numbers had six orders apiece, though three of those were consolidated into a single case.

The counsel section of each written opinion was then coded to identify the attorneys that presented oral argument. For each attorney I noted: any title by which they were identified, their role (i.e. counsel for petitioner, counsel for respondent, counsel for *amicus*), and the names of any other attorneys identified as being with them "on the briefs." Across the 146 cases in my sample, 343 oral arguments by counsel were presented for an average of 2.35 per docket number. The most attorneys arguing in any one case was four. On average, 2.58 other attorneys were listed as being on the brief, with seventeen being the maximum.

Based upon names and titles, I determined that these 343 oral arguments were presented by 260 different attorneys. For each attorney, I attempted to locate information of primary usefulness in determining their comparative experience, including the law school they attended, whether they clerked for a member of the Supreme Court, and their prior experience as an oral advocate before the Court.[41] When possible, I recorded additional data about the attorneys that might aid in identification or that might prove helpful for future research.[42]

Gathering this information for the 1979 term required a number of sources, including the current electronic Martindale-Hubbell Law Directory offered by LexisNexis, supplemented by general web searches.[43] After exhausting electronic resources, I was left with over

---

[41] Some studies of attorney experience have included a variable to measure whether the attorney was a practicing law professor at the time of the argument (c.f. McGuire 1993). In their 2007 piece examining Justice Blackmun's oral argument grades, Johnson, Spriggs, and Wahlbeck found that their law professor variable did not appear to be significantly related to measures of attorney experience (Johnson et al. 2007, 23). For that reason, I have not included a separate measure of professorship. This study also does not currently include a variable to measure whether attorneys are part of the "elite" Washington, D.C. appellate bar. For more information on measuring attorney experience, please see Lazarus 2008.

[42] Information included International Standards Lawyer Number (ISLN), years of birth and death, date of first bar admission, college attended, college and law school graduation dates, degrees earned, academic honors received, and any other potentially relevant biographical data.

[43] Some individuals proved fairly easy to identify. A web search for Louis Claiborne, for example, reveals his New York Times obituary which includes

60 attorneys for whom I had no details whatsoever, as well as many that I wanted to verify more fully. For these individuals I turned to the print edition of the Martindale-Hubbell Law Directory.[44]

The remaining data about attorneys were, comparatively, easier to come by. Details on clerking experience were taken from the appendix to Peppers' *Courtiers of the Marble Place,* which contains a list of all the individuals clerking for the Court between 1882 and 2004 (Peppers 2006). Of the attorneys arguing before the Court in 1979, a full twenty had previously clerked for a justice. Finally, an attorney's prior experi-

---

his attendance at Tulane University Law School. In all honesty, of course, a Deputy Solicitor General should be fairly easy to find. A more typical example might be Robert K. Best, who argued for respondent in *Costle and Environmental Protection Agency v. Pacific Legal Foundation et Al. (*445 U.S. 198). This case was Best's first. He would not appear before the Court again until 1987 in *Nollan v. California Coastal Commission* (483 U.S. 825)—his only other time before the Court. I located Best's educational information when a web search turned up his of counsel profile page on the website of Trainor Fairbrook, Attorneys at Law.

[44] With roots stretching back to the 1860s, Martindale-Hubbell publishes perhaps the most complete listing of attorneys, including practice locations and educational background. Because of the sheer volume of information, few libraries carry material backdated to the period I needed. The nearest library with copies of the directory reaching back to the 1970s was the University of Michigan Law Library. I had initially hoped to be able to gather these data from microfiche copies of the Directory. Because the collection spans dozens of fiche, the University of Michigan was reluctant to send them through Inter-Library Loan—requiring a visit in person to Ann Arbor.

Complicating this research was one major factor: the directory is organized geographically. I could fairly easily locate attorneys whose location I had prior knowledge of. For many, though, I needed to search through the collective index that Martindale-Hubbell publishes periodically. Unfortunately, the index in the University library closest to the 1979 term was the 1993 index. Due to library policy, rather than pouring through the microfiche for the 1979 directory, it was easier to start by reviewing the next-closest print copies that the library maintained in its closed stacks. Any attorneys not located in print editions of the Directory I then searched for in the 1979 Directory microfiche, using as many geographic clues as I could gather. At the end of my day in the library, I was left with six attorneys whose educational background I could not ascertain. I was able to locate a current phone number for one attorney, James I. Meyerson, and briefly interviewed him as to relevant details. Another attorney, F. Randall Karfonta, was listed in Martindale-Hubbell but had no law school listed. A phone call to his office elicited an unexpectedly hostile and non-cooperative response.

ence before the Court was determined in what has become the conventional manner: searching Lexis/Nexis for cases in which attorneys of the same name were listed as arguing a case (c.f. Johnson, Spriggs, and Wahlbeck 2007, 17).[45] In gathering this data I recorded both the number of cases argued prior to the case in question, as well as the total number of cases argued up to the present.[46] The mean level of prior litigating experience, as of the time of the 1979 appearance, was 4.86 cases, with a standard deviation of 12.22; the most cases argued by any single attorney was 97 (Erwin Griswold), and the median number of cases argued was 0. These numbers generally parallel those in Roberts 2005.

The Role of Experience

If the experience of counsel itself impacts the presence of *amici* at oral argument, this connection could be found in any or all of my three experience-related variables (prior arguments, elite law school attendance, and clerkship). To capture the cumulative effect of multiple counsel presenting argument for a particular side, after calculating each attorney's prior oral argument experience, Supreme Court clerking, and attendance at elite law schools, I aggregate these scores for all the attorneys arguing on a particular side.[47]

Following Johnson et al. 2006, I begin with the natural log of each attorney's prior number of appearances before the Court.[48] If multiple attorneys presented argument on a given side, then I take the natural log of the sum of their prior appearances. The average experience value for

---

[45] Because of the non-standardization of Court and legal records, this method is the best available but clearly has its flaws. While matches are initially made based upon name, other biographical data must frequently be used to verify or rule out possible matches. There also remains the possibility that two attorneys whose names appear to be identical are in fact different individuals. For another statement on the difficulty that judicial scholars have in properly identifying attorneys, see McGuire 1998, 513–4.

[46] While this number is of no direct relevance for the research in this chapter, it seemed prudent to save this information in order to prepare for future research.

[47] Of course, I exclude from each side's experience—as well as clerking and law school measures—any counsel appearing on that side's behalf as an *amicus curiae*.

[48] In short, the natural log of experience is a useful way to address the level of skew present in the number of prior arguments presented by counsel. See note 36 above. Before taking the natural log, 1 is added to each attorneys experience to compensate for the fact that the natural log of 0 is undefined.

counsel arguing for the case's first party is .948, with a standard deviation of 1.247 and a range between 0 and 4.585. Attorneys for the second party have a mean experience of .656, with a standard deviation of .974 and a range between 0 and 4.094. Having clerked for a Supreme Court justice and attended an elite law school are treated similarly—as a dichotomous dummy variable for each attorney, with the scores for all attorneys on a given side added together. Summary statistics for all these variables are presented in Table 2.1. I then measure the overall level of experience in a case, creating variables for the average prior argument appearances of both parties, their average clerkship, and elite law school attendance. I expect these variables to be negatively correlated with the presence of oral *amici.* This would indicate that as a case features lower levels of attorney experience, it becomes more likely to have oral *amici*. Summary statistics for these experience variables can be found in Table 2.2.

Table 2.1: Descriptive Statistics for Aggregate Experience Variables

	MEAN	STD DEV	MIN	MAX
Prior Arguments	.802	.839	0	3.267
Clerkship	.106	.236	0	1
Elite Law School	.428	.435	0	2

Table 2.2: Descriptive Statistics for Attorney Experience Variables

		MEAN	STD DEV	MIN	MAX
Clerkship	*Overall*	.106	.330	0	2
	Party 1	.116	.343	0	2
	Party 2	.096	.318	0	2
Elite Law School	*Overall*	.428	.555	0	3
	Party 1	.445	.526	0	2
	Party 2	.411	.583	0	3
Prior Arguments	*Overall*	.802	1.126	0	4.585
	Party 1	.948	1.247	0	4.585
	Party 2	.656	.974	0	4.094

To control for the variety of factors that could be at work, multivariate regression analysis would be the best approach. However, with only one term's worth of data, the generally rare occurrence of oral amici, and the sheer number of possible independent variables, a less igorous method is needed.[49] Tables 2.3, 2.4, and 2.5 show the crosstabulations for the three attorney variables compared to the presence of oral amici. Standard measures of significance and association are reported with each table.

Of the three variables, only prior argument experience appears to have a significant relationship with oral amici; the chi-squares for the clerkship variable and the elite schooling variable both fall below accepted thresholds. Cramér's V, a measure of the strength of a relationship, shows that the connection between arguments and oral amici is fairly strong. For this reason, I believe it is tentatively possible to accept the Collective Experience Hypothesis as outline above.

---

[49] As an experiment, I used the 1979 data to run a logistic regression model. The dichotomous dependent variable reflected whether the case had any oral *amici* at the level of individual docket numbers; this variable indicates the general presence or oral *amici* regardless of which side they appear on. As controls I included a number of standard variables that matched the case demographics description above; these variables are the same as those found in Chapter 3. In no variation of the model did either measure achieve significance.
Other measures for lower court dissent or conflict among Courts of Appeals failed to achieve significance. A dummy variable for the presence of an issue of constitutional provision or an amendment was in fact significant and signed as would be expected. The presence of *amici*, measured as the natural logarithm of the number of briefs, leads to a variable that is significant even with cert *amici* included. Variables about case complexity and the role of the Solicitor General approach significance, and would likely show better results with an expanded dataset.
When it comes to attorney experience, not all measures of experience appear to be effective. Two of the three averaged experience variables are not significant; neither prior clerkship nor attendance at an elite law school—or at least a measure that averages those traits collected by party—has a discernable impact. Only prior argument experience rises to statistical significance.

Table 2.3: Crosstabulation of Argument Experience on the Presence of Oral *Amici*

HAS ORAL *AMICI*	LEVEL OF PRIOR ARGUMENT EXPERIENCE[A] None	Low	High	Total
No	37 (74)	49 (92)	41 (95)	127 (87)
Yes	13 (26)	4 (8)	2 (5)	19 (13)
Total	50 (100)	53 (100)	43 (100)	146 (100)

$Chi^2 = 11.504$; $p = .003$
Cramér's V = .281

* Percentages, in parentheses, are in-column percents.

[a] Categories are based on the average number of prior arguments for the parties' attorneys, based on a logarithmic scale. The "none" category represents all cases where neither side had prior experience. The cut-off point for "low" experience was 1.2, with the "high" category representing all other levels of experience.

Table 2.4: Crosstabulation of Elite Schooling on the Presence of Oral *Amici*

HAS ORAL *AMICI*	ELITE LAW SCHOOLING, AVERAGE[A] None	Low	High	Total
No	50 (85)	46 (84)	31 (97)	127 (87)
Yes	9 (15)	9 (16)	1 (3)	19 (13)
Total	59 (100)	55 (100)	32 (100)	146 (100)

$Chi^2 = 3.571$; $p = .168$
Cramér's V = .156

* Percentages, in parentheses, are in-column percents.

[a] Categories are based on the average elite law school attendance. The "none" category represents all cases where neither side had elite training. The cut-off point for "low" was 0.5, with the "high" category representing all other levels of elite schooling.

Table 2.5: Crosstabulation of SCOTUS Clerkship on the Presence of Oral *Amici*

Has Oral *Amici*	Clerkship, Average[A] None	Low	High	Total
No	102 (85)	21 (91)	4 (100)	127 (87)
Yes	17 (15)	2 (9)	0 (0)	19 (13)
Total	119 (100)	23 (100)	4 (100)	146 (100)

$Chi^2 = 1.147$; $p = .563$
Cramér's V = .089

* Percentages, in parentheses, are in-column percents.

[a] Categories are based on the average Supreme Court clerkship of the parties in a case. The "none" category represents all cases where neither side had clerked for a Justice. The "low" category represents the averaged value of 0.5, and the "high" category representing the averaged value of 1.

Table 2.6: Comparison of 1979 Term with Whole Dataset

	1953–1985	**1979**
Total Cases	4635	147
Cases with Oral *Amici*	347 (7.49%)	19 (12.93%)
Total *Amicus* Appearances	433	19
Average Appearances per Case	1.25	1
Single Shot *Amici*	62 (72.09%)	4 (80%)
Repeat *Amici*	24 (27.91%)	1 (20%)
Appearances per *Amici*	5.03	3.8
Appearances by United States as *Amicus*	276 (63.74%)	15 (78.95%)

ORAL AMICI: A QUALITATIVE LOOK

Between the years of 1953 and 1985, a total of 433 *amici* presented oral argument before the Court, spread across 347 different cases. The size of this number masks the influence of *amici* who made repeat appearances. While sixty-two groups presented argument on only one occasion, twenty-four groups had multiple appearances. The mean number of appearances across these terms was five cases per group—a number heavily skewed by the fact that the United States government alone accounted for 276 appearances. The two next most frequent a*mici* were the Securities and Exchange Commission and the State of California, with 19 and 13 appearances respectively.

As Table 2.6 shows, the 1979 term was fairly normal. A slightly higher than average proportion of cases had oral *amici*. Similarly, the percentage of appearances by "single shot" *amici* was above average. And even though the United States was the only repeat *amicus* during the term, it also had a slightly higher than average presence. The 1979 term is also distinct in that it had no cases with multiple oral *amici*.

In order to provide a more complete picture of the role of oral *amici*, this chapter concludes with a set of descriptive case studies of three cases from the 1979 term: one in which the United States participated as an *amicus*, and the two other cases where the *amici* were not the federal government. The details of each case and their oral argument will first be presented, and then I will draw conclusions about oral *amici* across all three cases.[50]

Mobil Oil Corporation v. Commissioner of Taxes of Vermont

On November 7, 1979, the Supreme Court heard arguments in a case that touched upon the nature of multistate corporations, the states' power to tax, and the Constitution's commerce clause and due process requirements. As a result of what it believed to be overtaxation of its income within the state, Mobil Oil Corporation filed suit against Vermont. At the heart of the dispute was income that the company had earned from dividends in certain stocks of subsidiary companies. Some of these subsidiaries were domestic companies that operated entirely

---

[50] The decision as to which cases appear in the following sections was neither a random nor a purposeful choice. Given that many cases featured the United States as *amicus*, I chose several cases because they featured private third parties. However, transcripts were not available for every case, limiting my options somewhat. Given its uniqueness in the term, I had wanted in particular to include *California Retail Liquor Dealers Association v. Midcal Aluminum, Inc., et al* (445 U.S. 97), since it features a state deputy attorney general appearing as *amicus*. This was, unfortunately, one of the cases without a transcript readily available.

overseas, and some were foreign-organized companies that operated overseas.

Mobil's claim was that this foreign-source income might have been taxable in its corporate home state of New York, but was not in other states. Correspondingly, when the company completed its Vermont income tax returns for the years 1970 through 1972, it excluded from its taxable income its foreign dividends. Vermont's tax commissioner recalculated the company's taxable income and assessed its taxes on the full value of its income—which was, across the three years, underreported by an average of $245 million per year.[51] When the company's appeal to the tax commissioner failed, it filed suit in the Superior Court of Washington County. After said court reversed the commissioner's ruling, the state prevailed in its own appeal to the Supreme Court of Vermont. Mobil's loss there and its constitutional claims brought the case to the Supreme Court.

The *Mobil* case is a fairly good exemplar for cases with oral *amici.* By most traditional measures, it was not likely to excite public attention. Two constitutional claims were at stake, but neither had much bearing on the average American. The case was never featured on the *New York Times* front page and came directly from the Vermont Supreme Court, without any suggestion that lower federal appeals courts were in conflict. The Solicitor General neither was invited nor sought to participate in the case. All that aside, there was interest in the case within the appropriate communities. Two groups filed motions to participate as *amici* prior to the decision to note jurisdiction; both the National Association of Manufacturers and the Committee on State Taxation of the Council of State Chambers of Commerce received Mobil's permission to participate as *amici* but were denied by Vermont.[52] The Court granted leave to both groups.

When briefs were filed on the merits, four more groups joined the case. One, the Multistate Tax Commission, would go on to share time at oral arguments. The Commission's brief supporting Vermont was

---

[51] Blackmun's majority opinion notes that for the three years, Mobil's federal taxable income was $220 million, $308 million, and $233 million. Of those figures, $174 million, $283 million, and $280 million was divided income (445 U.S. 430).

[52] The National Association of Manufacturers ultimately urged reversal in its brief. The brief for the Committee on State Taxation notes its support for appellants, although the case's syllabus notes the *amicus'* presence without an indication of which party it supported.

signed by thirteen other states and their Attorneys General. Also siding with the appellees were the states of Illinois, Connecticut, Massachusetts, and New Hampshire—together on one brief—and the Standard Oil Company of California. The County of Los Angeles also participated as *amicus*. Though its brief does not take a side in the matter, its goal was to note that Mobil's due process and commerce clause arguments would ultimately disadvantage the county's power to tax.

Presenting the case for the appellant was Jerome R. Hellerstein. As a graduate of Harvard Law, he was the only one of the case's three oral advocates to have attended an elite law school. None were former clerks. Even though the *Mobil* case would be his only appearance before the high court, Hellerstein had a fairly distinguished career in the area of tax law. In addition to his private practice, he was a professor of law at New York University. With his son Walter he authored one of the leading texts on state taxation—the aptly named *State Taxation.*[53] Since transcripts of the period do not indicate the names of justices asking questions, it is somewhat difficult to determine how broadly the Court questioned Hellerstein. Based on his references to members of the Court by name, he received questions from Rehnquist, Blackmun, White, and Stevens at the least. Given that Stewart and Marshall took no part in the case, he was asked questions by more than half of the justices who were sitting.

From a transcript alone it is hard to determine the tone in which questions were asked. The content of the justices' questions, at least, suggest a Court that was receptive to Hellerstein but definitely cautious about the implications of Mobil's argument. After a few preparatory questions about the company's tax burden and Vermont's appeals process, the Court probed Hellerstein as to how Mobil's situation would be distinguished from a company in which the income from the subsidiaries simply flowed directly to the parent corporation, or from a company which solely used domestic subsidiaries to complete the corporation's work within certain states. Another line of questioning revealed a bit of

[53] Walter Hellerstein is himself a professor of law at the University of Georgia and has had perhaps an even more distinguished career than his father—if only measured by the fact the has argued two cases before the Court, compared to his father's one. Perhaps ironically, in 1992 the younger Hellerstein received the Multistate Tax Commission's 25th Anniversary Award for Outstanding Contributions to Multistate Taxation—the same Multistate Tax Commission that his father found himself arguing against when it appeared as *amicus* in the *Mobil* case.

frustration with Hellerstein's commerce clause argument; White and Rehnquist tried, not entirely to their satisfaction, to have counsel clarify why he would limit focus solely on the protection of foreign-source income under the clause when the language, as written, would seem to apply just as clearly to domestic interstate commerce. The most telling questioning of all came from Justice Stevens, the case's lone dissenter. Building off of elements of the other justices' questions—and noting in particular a question asked by Blackmun, the author of the Court's opinion—Stevens tried to gauge Hellerstein's opinion about a fictitious corporation which had an internal division whose business was entirely distinct from the parent corporation. Stevens suggested the possibility of an oil company like Mobil having a toy division. Hellerstein briefly answered the question by suggesting that no state would consider the divisions together under a unitary understanding of the company.

Like Hellerstein, the counsel for Vermont had no prior argument experience before the Court and would make *Mobil* his sole appearance. Richard Johnston King, though, had a fairly personal connection to the case and its circumstances. Although he was an associate at Debevoise, Plimpton, Lyon & Gates during the tax years disputed in the case, during the mid to late 1970s he would serve as Assistant Attorney General for the state, as General Counsel for the Department of Taxes, and then as Deputy and Acting Tax Commissioner. His wife Harriet Ann King was herself serving as Tax Commissioner while the *Mobil* case was being heard by the Court.

King began his presentation by reiterating Vermont's method for apportioning income, linking the state's formula to federally reported taxable income. As explained in his opening statement, the bedrock of his argument had two parts: neither of Mobil's constitutional claims validly require the exclusion of the dividends from income tax calculations, and the company had not met its burden of proving that the income from its subsidiaries was substantially unrelated to its integrated petroleum business. After laying out those basics, he was interrupted with much the same hypotheticals that had been offered to Hellerstein. At least on a reading of the transcript alone, his responses were much less adept. In response to Stevens' hypothetical toy business, King first criticized opposing counsel's answer on technical grounds. Only after multiple restatements of the question from the bench did he admit that Hellerstein's appraisal of the situation was likely correct and that Vermont's policies were shared by a minority of states. King similarly struggled with questions about hypothetical dividend income from stock held in an entirely separate company, such as DuPont, and with questions about the taxability of intangibles.

Whether the justices ultimately tired of the questioning, realized that his time was approaching an end, or were trying to lead King back to solid ground, the attorney ended his argument on a much stronger note. By my calculations, his last two responses to questions lasted some 770 and 400 words apiece. The only interruption he received was a brief question for clarification of a precedent cited by the appellant. This stands in contrast to the rest of his argument where—excluding introductory remarks—his longest uninterrupted speech was only 116 words. The content of those last two speeches seems to be pivotal for how the Court resolved the case. In his closing moments, King offered four main points. First, appellants had not met their burden of proof regarding why their foreign-source dividends should be excluded from Vermont's calculations; King also concluded with this claim. Second, King salvaged the discussion of taxing intangibles by making the argument that dividends are really no different from income made off of other intangibles, which no one had argued should be excluded.[54] Third, given that Mobil had been arguing for what was seen as a "novel" concept of taxation, King restated that both the courts and the states had long ago settled on apportionment as the fairest method for taxing income in situations like Mobil's. Finally, he summarized how the facts and available precedent did not support appellant's case.[55]

Unlike his fellow advocates, Dexter was no stranger to the Court's chambers. Two years prior to *Mobil*, he had personally appeared before the Court to argue about the validity of the Multistate Tax Commission itself—the *amicus* he was representing in *Mobil*.[56] Some twenty years before that, he had also argued on behalf of the state of Michigan in a stock and bank taxation case.[57] In both of these prior appearances, he

[54] His chief examples are patents and royalties, where the income generated is rightly taxable but the underlying "property" is not taxable, at lest on an income basis.

[55] Chief here was the fact that while Mobil's arguments rested on avoiding multiple taxation, no such taxation had actually occurred—and, if it had, there was an appropriate appeals process in place for resolving it in a fair manner. King also cut to the heart of Hellerstein's foreign commerce argument by noting that Court precedent had never held income from income from foreign commerce was the same as foreign commerce itself.

[56] *U.S. Steel Corp v. Multistate Tax Commission*, 434 U.S. 452 (1978).

[57] *Michigan National Bank v. Michigan*, 365 U.S. 467 (1961).

was on the winning side. All in all, Dexter would argue five cases before the Supreme Court and would lose only one.[58]

Because of his prior appearances before the Court and his close connection to the issue of multi-state taxation, Dexter had as much claim to be an expert in this case as anyone. He began his argument by focusing on the settled standards for taxing intangible property and the novelty of Mobil's claims in the case. As had happened with the two prior attorneys, though, the debate quickly switched to Stevens' hypothetical toy business.[59] Dexter was ultimately forced to admit that a valid due process claim would exist in the case of a unitary domestic business where an entirely separate division, operating entirely outside of Vermont, were to have its income taxed by Vermont. Having done so, Dexter quickly tries to separate that hypothetical case from the one under consideration.

The Court's questions then turned towards the actual operation of the three-factor apportionment formula used by Vermont and other states. Under the system, states determined what percentage of a corporation's income to tax by looking at the company's overall sales, payroll, and property values, dividing each by the amount that occurs within the state, and then averaging together those three fractions. The general consensus was that this system was best equipped to reasonably tax a corporation whose business and income crossed borders in a way that defied simple allocation to one state or another. With a three factor system, a company's state tax liability can change in several ways. First, as the company's net income increases so too will the tax it pays to the state at the given calculated apportionment. Second, if the value of the company's sales, payroll, or property in the state increases, then

---

58 *Bacchus Imports Limited v. Dias*, 468 U.S. 263 (1984).

59 The reasons for Stevens' focus on this hypothetical appear to be effectively summarized in his dissent in the case. Central to his disagreement with the rest of the Court was the question of whether Mobil's subsidiaries should really be considered part and parcel of its unitary, integrated business. The Court's opinion, written by Blackmun, takes as a given that Mobil failed to show that its dividend income was *not* part of its unitary business. Stevens worries less about this factual question and instead suggests that Vermont is seeking to apply its three-factor apportionment formula in a discriminatory manner. If the state wanted to tax all the corporation's income inclusive of subsidiary dividends, it should then also be consistent by including the subsidiaries' property, sales, and payroll in the formula—as would be appropriate if they were to truly be considered part of the unitary business.

the apportionment percentage will also increase. Finally, an increase in overall sales, payroll, or property will tend to decrease the apportionment factor as long as the state's share does not increase as well.

The logic of this method was tested when the Court began asking why the value of the stocks that generated the suspect dividends was not included in the property factor component of Vermont's apportionment calculation.[60] In a somewhat tense interchange with the Court, Dexter fell back on the fact that historically three-factor formulas only took tangible property into account; because such assets could not be physically located in order to be placed into the numerator of the "property factor," their value could not be included in the denominator of the fraction either. This clearly did not satisfy the Court, which pointed out that when it comes to the denominator—total corporate property—Vermont really knows and cares little about where tangible property is located; all the state wants to know is the total value of the property. Dexter never conceded the Court's suggestion that the value of the stocks should be included in the property factor, but he did ultimately understand what the Court was driving at. Including the stocks without attributing any of it to the state's property numerator would clearly decrease the apportionment factor and lower the company's tax burden, regardless of whether dividend income was taxed or not. When the Court asked if the state would like such a change to its calculations, Dexter responds "No, I doubt it."

The Court offered Hellerstein time for a rebuttal. After making a few general remarks, the counsel for Mobil was also given the question about including stock value in the state's apportionment calculations. Though he agreed that such a system would be preferable to the status quo, he failed to take the bait. In the longest speech of his rebuttal, Hellerstein returns to the argument that dividends must be treated differently from normal income, which the apportionment method was designed to handle. The remainder of his rebuttal was spent answering

---

[60] Relying on transcripts alone, it is impossible to determine which justices were involved in this questioning. Given the similarity to issues raised in Stevens' dissent, it seems likely that most of the questions asked here were his. This section of the transcript, though, is introduced by a reference to a question posed by Justice White. Unfortunately, the transcript notes that the reference in question ends in "illegible words."

brief hypotheticals about the actual application of Mobil's plan for the taxation of dividends.[61]

Village of Schaumburg v. Citizens for a Better Environment et al.

Unlike *Mobil*, the Schaumburg case was likely to generate broad public interest.[62] Coming out of what was then a village on the edge of metropolitan Chicago, the case centered upon First Amendment free speech rights and the legitimate scope of local police power as permitted under the Fourteenth Amendment. Schaumburg had enacted a local ordinance designed to protect citizens from annoyance, fraud, and crime by requiring that groups interested in door-to-door solicitation receive a permit conditioned on showing that seventy-five percent of the contributions would go towards its stated charitable purpose.[63] That ordinance—along with those of other Chicagoland municipalities—was challenged by Citizens for a Better Environment (CBE), a non-profit group whose principal aim was to inform and educate the public on environmental issues. Throughout the proceedings, CBE was contrasted with so-called "traditional" charitable groups whose goal was to provide money or services to some population in need. CBE, on the other hand, existed in order to spread information. The money that the group raised was largely spent on paying the salaries of researchers, attorneys, and canvassers who developed and spread the group's position on the environment. Since such expenses regularly exceeded twenty-five percent of the group's spending, CBE was denied a permit to solicit in Schaumburg.

The case, started in Federal District Court, focused on the facial invalidity of the ordinance in light of the First and Fourteenth Amend-

[61] Mobil's plan was to have the types of dividends in question be taxable where the company had its corporate domicile. The Court asked Hellerstein about resolving situations where the corporate domicile was in question or where a company's commercial and corporate domiciles both wanted to tax dividends at 100%.

[62] A total of six *amici* ultimately participated in the case. All six had to petition the Court to participate, because Schaumburg not only denied them permission but went so far as to file an objection to the *amici*'s motions.

[63] The ordinance also applied to groups soliciting on public streets, but the door-to-door aspect was the focus of the case. The seventy-five percent requirement was written such that costs deemed to be related to the administration of the organization (e.g. salaries, advertising, legal fees, phone charges, etc.) could not exceed twenty-five percent of the group's contributions.

ments. The court granted CBE summary judgment, which was upheld by the Seventh Circuit Court of Appeals.[64] One of Schaumburg's claims in the case was that summary judgment was not appropriate, and that by so ruling the lower court had failed to develop a satisfactory factual record about the nature of CBE's activities. The Supreme Court granted certiorari in the case in April 1979, at the end of the 1978 term, and heard arguments at the end of October.

Representing the Village of Schaumburg was Jack M. Siegel. A graduate of the University of Chicago Law School,[65] Siegel served as attorney or special counsel for a variety of villages and cities around Chicago. He also was the author of Schaumburg's solicitation ordinance. In his capacity as attorney for Arlington Heights, Siegel appeared before the Supreme Court in 1976 when the village's planning commission was charged with violating the Fourteenth Amendment's Equal Protection Clause by preventing the development of racially-diverse higher-density residential developments. The Court ultimately sided with Siegel and Arlington Heights.

Arguing in *Schaumburg*, Siegel began with a statement of the history of the case. His discussion of the District Court's summary judgment elicited several routine questions from the Court about the nature of the judgment and the basis for the lower court's ruling. Since the original case had been filed against nearly two dozen municipalities, one question focused on how Schaumburg's ordinance compared to others in northern Illinois. The chief difference in Siegel's mind is that while other cities and villages placed permit-granting power under the discretion of an administrative officer, Schaumburg's seventy-five percent requirement was a neutral, mandatory guideline. By drafting the law in those terms, the goal had been to avoid the Supreme Court's well-known concern with the arbitrary discretion of public officials.[66]

Despite Siegel's pride on that point, the Court was interested in other matters. To answer a question about why the village set its requirement at seventy-five percent, Siegel referred to a case from the Fifth Circuit Court of Appeals. Decided in 1969, *National Foundation*

---

[64] The Court of Appeals did disagree with the District Court about the question of the ordinance's facial validity, holding that it was simply unconstitutional as applied.

[65] For purposes of the analysis in the first half of this chapter, the University of Chicago is considered an elite law school.

[66] See, for example, *Cantwell v. Connecticut*, 310 U.S. 296 (1940).

v. City of Fort Worth held that a municipality could deny a solicitation permit when the cost of solicitation itself was deemed to be excessive; Ft. Worth had set its limit at eighty percent (415 F.2d 41).[67] Testing the reasonableness of the figure, the Court asked if the village's argument would change had the number been ninety percent. A fair interpretation of this line of questioning might be that Schaumburg's ordinance had been designed to avoid one form of arbitrariness but had fallen afoul of another. Perhaps sensing this, Siegel sought to change the Court's focus from the freedom of speech to the exercise of local police power. Three factors justified the type of ordinance that Schaumburg passed: the local community's desire to protect its citizens from physical danger, annoyance in their homes, and from fraud. While the Court would return to these issues, he was unable to redirect the justices.

The first hypothetical Siegel faced struck at the 75/25 split in expenses laid out by the ordinance. According to the text, advertising expenses were to be counted in the twenty-five percent. The Court asked Siegel to imagine how the ordinance would be applied to a group whose sole charitable purpose was to advertise and spread information. All the group's funds—one hundred percent—would be spent on advertising. Given that Citizens for a Better Environment claimed to operate along those lines, the hypothetical was especially pertinent.[68] For anyone already suspicious of the village's motives, Siegel's bobbled response would have failed to change anything. Initially he suggested that a group whose sole purpose was advertising would have been allowed a solicitation permit. Another question from the bench, though, challenged that interpretation and suggested that the text of the ordinance itself demanded the permit be denied. After attempting to distinguish between advertising tied to solicitation and administrative expenses, versus advertising for public education, Siegel faced several questions about how Illinois state courts had interpreted statutes like the one in question.

---

[67] Though a decision of the Fifth Circuit would clearly not have much precedential value in the Seventh Circuit, where Schaumburg was situated, Siegel was clearly relying upon the fact that the Supreme Court had denied certiorari in the Ft. Worth case—leaving in place the Court of Appeals' ruling on the validity of the ordinance.

[68] As would become clear in the arguments of respondent's counsel and the *amicus*, the real question for the case seemed to come down to whether the active solicitation for funds could be sufficiently separated from the task of spreading information to render one activity permitted and the other not.

After seeming to be on the defensive for most of this argument, Siegel gained a bit of rest when one of the justices helpfully observed that the ordinance only applied to situations involving solicitation; a group who only wanted to go door-to-door and spread information would not even need to apply for a permit. Separating the issue in this manner allowed Siegel to return to his argument about valid local police power. In his words, the village had no interest in limiting speech or advocacy of any kind, but was chiefly concerned about solicitors who went around raising funds for charities but actually kept a large portion of the money raised. While their counsel also emphasized the issues of personal safety and homeowner annoyance, the heart of Schaumburg's logic was the prevention of fraud.

Unfortunately, dividing the issue in this manner left Siegel with two difficult claims to defend. The first was his statement that the First Amendment offers absolutely no protection for door-to-door solicitation. The Court directed Siegel's attention to prior cases that had protected something akin to the solicitation at stake—especially cases involving the Jehovah's Witnesses. Counsel argued that a clear difference could be seen between CBE's solicitation and the Witnesses' exercise of their religious freedom combined with solicitation. When at least one member of the Court failed to accept his distinction, Siegel retreated to a restatement of the limited precedents that supported the village's focus on privacy, annoyance, and fraud.

After the Court pointed out that the ordinance did little to protect privacy or prevent annoyance, since the village was willing to allow essentially unlimited door-to-door canvassing as long as no soliciting was involved, Siegel suddenly became a fan of the First Amendment. Claiming that at least some annoyance had to be accepted under the right to free speech, he turned in the end to the question of fraud. This may have seemed like solid ground, but here Siegel had an equally difficult claim to make: namely that the ordinance, as adopted by Schaumburg, was a fair and reasonable way to identify fraud. The Court's questioning began to take on an increasingly skeptical tone as the justices asked Siegel how the seventy-five percent figure had been reached, as well as whether the village had made any effort to determine how many groups would be disadvantaged by the ordinance. When the Court went so far to ask, perhaps facetiously, if Schaumburg had simply wanted the highest figure it could get, Siegel quickly wrapped up his argument and asked to reserve the remainder of his time.

Siegel and his opposing counsel were well matched. Milton I. Shadur was also a graduate of the "elite" University of Chicago Law School. While Shadur had also not clerked for a member of the Supreme Court, in his one prior appearance before the Court he had as co-counsel future Court member Arthur J. Goldberg.[69] Shadur himself would ultimately make his way to the bench. In 1980, President Carter appointed him to the U.S. District Court for the Northern District of Illinois, a position he still holds to this day.

Shadur began his argument by briefly touching on Schaumburg's claim that summary judgment had been inappropriate in the case. While that point had been an important aspect of Siegel's case, the Court was not interested in exploring it with Shadur either. Instead, they returned to the question of whether solicitation itself deserved any protection under the First Amendment. Testing him with an extreme hypothetical, the Court asked Shadur if he believed a total ban on all solicitation would be constitutional. After trying to limit his response to situations involving groups like CBE, he had to admit—albeit, with the Court's prompting—that even traditional charities would be challenged by such a law. Shadur went on to claim that a total ban would violate the spirit of the Court's precedents, even though the only prohibited behavior was soliciting itself. In response to a question, he did admit that it would be perfectly acceptable for individual homeowners to prohibit solicitation on their own property via posted signs.

From the questions that followed, it seems clear that the justices wanted to probe Shadur's presuppositions a bit more. In particular, the Court repeatedly asked him for any available precedent to support his claim that solicitation deserved protection. Without any clearly identifiable cases to offer, Shadur tweaked the issue slightly. Solicitation by itself might deserve protection. But in the case of charities, solicitation is always joined with some other purpose which itself is protected under the First Amendment. After a few marginally-answered hypotheticals about door-to-door sales of magazines and stocks (which Shadur tried to suggest are clearly commercial speech and beyond the case's purview), the questioning returned to fact that the ordinance only forbade solicitation, not expressive speech. When asked in particular about the validity of the seventy-five percent threshold, CBE's counsel was able to briefly switch from defense to offense. At the end of petitioner's argument, the Court had turned skeptical about Schaumburg's ordi-

---

[69] *Government Employees v. Windsor*, 353 U.S. 364 (1957).

nance. Shadur directly played off those concerns. Setting an arbitrary seventy-five percent requirement ignored the unpredictable costs that groups often face in their early years of operation, where administrative overhead can be unusually high. He also detailed how Schaumburg's ordinance explicitly deviated from the Illinois solicitation statute in its categorization of solicitation expenses.[70]

A sudden and perhaps unexpected question moved the discussion in the direction of permissible police powers. One justice asked whether CBE had sought permission to solicit under the for-profit provisions of the Schaumburg ordinance. Shadur answered that they had not, since the group was not organized for profit. Without being bidden, he then took the extra step of suggesting that those provisions should also have been declared unconstitutional, since permits for commercial solicitation were to be issued on the discretion of the chief of police. In the mind of at least one justice, Shadur had just painted himself into a corner. Given the anonymity of this era's transcripts, it is impossible to know who asked the question. The concern, however, is clear:

> "Well, you say, in effect, then, there's no way that a municipal corporation can accomplish the result that they want to accomplish here. They can't do it by lodging discretion in the chief of police, and they can't do it by the objective profile that they've attempted to do under Article I. You're saying, in effect, that people can come around and solicit money, and that there's simply nothing they can do about it." (Oyez *Schaumburg*)

While it is hard to say if Shadur realized he was walking into a trap or not, he clearly took issue with this characterization of his claim. After a brief verbal tussle with the justice about how to interpret his statement, Shadur attempted to salvage his point by directing the Court's attention to the various options that were available. If a municipality were concerned with fraud or privacy, local trespassing laws

---

[70] Shadur's examples included the salaries paid to canvassers, staff researchers, and attorneys. Under the Schaumburg law—but not apparently under the state statute—such expenses had to be contained in the twenty-five percent, even though these might be some of the largest expenses for a non-traditional charity.

and fraud statutes would be perfectly adequate to the task. Made clear in several follow-up questions, Shadur's argument rested on the distinction that in a situation like that of the case, communal judgment could not be substituted for the choices of individual citizens.

These claims might have dovetailed nicely with the Court's apparent concern about how Schaumburg went about protecting its citizens. Unfortunately for Shadur, the effect was to bring back the albatross that had been haunting him all argument: whether the First Amendment protected solicitation in and of itself. Once again, counsel tried to avoid the issue but was forced to answer by the Court. Picking apart the claim that non-traditional charities had their speech rights almost inextricably tied to solicitation, the Court asked if traditional groups like the Red Cross would have standing to challenge a hypothetical law banning all solicitation. To save his argument, Shadur suggested that traditional charities, when fundraising, participated in an activity with speech components. This effectively eliminated the functional distinction between traditional and nontraditional groups. It did not, though, end the questioning. In an interesting admission that was not explored further, Shadur conceded that he was effectively identifying two First Amendment interests: soliciting for funds itself, and the soliciting that makes possible the advocacy of information.

The end of Shadur's argument moved towards hypotheticals derived from the contention that solicitation deserved protection. In making his claims about First Amendment protection, Shadur suggested that there were clear differences between the charitable group that solicited donations to fund its education efforts and the for-profit group that simply sold goods or services. While the former should be protected, the latter constituted commercial speech and could be far more regulated. Either out of skepticism or for clarification, the Court asked how Shadur would respond to three different situations: a boy wandering a neighborhood to get donations to help finance his college costs, a gas station employee soliciting money to publish a book he wrote, and a potential candidate for office raising money door-to-door. In each case, Shadur argued that the solicitation in question should be protected. When he was asked if he would protect the same college-bound student were he raising money selling magazines, Shadur declined by suggesting that such an example would constitute commercial speech.

Before the Court could interrogate him further, he passed the baton to counsel for his *amicus*.[71]

Adam Yarmolinsky, attorney for the Coalition of National Voluntary Organizations et al.,[72] was a rookie at the Court and would only argue the one case in his career. By almost every other measure, however, he was above average. An undergraduate at Harvard and a law student at Yale, he went on to clerk for Justice Stanley Reed. During his professional career he played an important role in the Department of Defense under both Kennedy and Johnson, served on LBJ's Anti-Poverty Task Force and Carter's Arms Control and Disarmament Agency, taught at Harvard, and became provost at the University of Maryland. The group he was arguing for in *Schaumburg*, the Coalition of National Voluntary Organizations, filed a brief on behalf of its member organizations, many of whom were also co-signers. In its filing, the group echoed several of the respondent's claims. The CNVO's chief addition to the case, though, was the argument that when local municipalities enact such particular solicitation provisions, charitable groups that operate on a national basis become especially disadvantaged by the "patchwork" of local regulations that develops.

Yarmolinsky began his argument by offering two brief points: first, that Schaumburg's ordinance disadvantaged charities of all forms, and second that the fundraising of national-level charitable groups experienced a chilling effect due to patchwork regulations. Interrupting only to clarify why he focused on national groups, the Court allowed Yarmolinsky to continue for some time. Counsel's reiteration of points made by the respondents was stopped when he was asked several hypotheticals about modified versions of Schaumburg's ordinance. Yarmolinsky answered that there would be no constitutional objection to an ordinance requiring groups to inform home owners about their prior financial year's expenses—provided that it made exceptions for newly formed groups.[73] He also endorsed a version that would require solici-

[71] There are almost no clues throughout *Schaumburg's* transcript that would allow one to identify the justices asking questions. However, given that Rehnquist's dissent in the case argued that the Court would force on municipalities the impossible task of drawing distinctions between permitted and non-permitted solicitation, it seems reasonable that many of the final questions asked of Shadur came from Rehnquist. C.f. 444 U.S. 642

[72] CNVO's brief was co-signed by thirty-three different groups.

[73] Neither Yarmolinsky nor the Court made much of it, but after noting that he would have no First Amendment objections to the hypotheticals, the attorney

tors to inform the public about how much they personally earned while fundraising. One final hypothetical concerned the validity of an ordinance restricting solicitation to a limited number of evening hours. After confusing the substance of the question, Yarmolinsky vaguely suggested that such an ordinance might not be reasonable and then noted that his time was up.

Rather than let him off the hook, however, the Court continued to question Yarmolinsky. Having tested how he responded to various less restrictive versions of Schaumburg's ordinance, the Court turned the attorney's attention to the issues brought up in the parties' arguments. Chief Justice Burger asked whether he was advocating an unlimitable right to solicit funds, except from individuals who expressly forbid it (i.e. via a "no soliciting" sign). Yarmolinsky's response introduces an interesting dichotomy with the respondents. Shadur had advanced such a right and would have extended it to certain individual cases, such as the boy headed to college. Counsel for the *amicus* explicitly said those instances would be beyond protection, limiting solicitation rights to individuals operating on behalf of a charity. Quite logically, the Court followed up by noting that the First Amendment makes no reference to charities. Yarmolinsky's response is marginal at best, referring to the recognized validity of some limitations on First Amendment rights and the potential invalidity of Congress' denial of tax deductions for charitable contributions to individuals.

Siegel's rebuttal on behalf of the petitioner reflected something of an attempt to address the issues brought up throughout the arguments—pressing the point that respondents were seeking an unrestricted right to solicit funds without any prior precedent supporting their cause. He also quickly disposed of Yarmolinsky's patchwork claim by suggesting that such situations are entirely ordinary in our system of government, where statutory authority rests at several levels. A question from the bench asked for Siegel's response to an outright ban on charitable solicitation. While suggesting that there would be no explicit First Amendment problem with such a law, Siegel attempted to divert the Court by suggesting that there was no need to decide such an issue at the time.

To soften the blow of his absolute position, Siegel reiterated that he had nothing against the particular charities soliciting in Schaumburg.

---

commented that there may be problems with determining the proper level of government at which to enact such regulations.

This brief demonstration of warmth lead to one of the stranger moments in the case. While the tone is difficult to read from the transcript alone, the Court surprised Siegel by suggesting, perhaps facetiously, that he objected to Girl Scout cookies. After Siegel metaphorically caught his breath, the Court suggested that the Girl Scouts would not be able to comply with Schaumburg's ordinance because of their need to purchase cookies, which would qualify as an administrative expense and conceivably exceed the allowed twenty-five percent of expenses.[74] Before he could give a coherent response to the question, he was asked to reaffirm his statement that a total ban on solicitation would be valid under the First Amendment. After doing so, Siegel concluded his rebuttal by revisiting concerns the Court raised at the end of his initial argument—namely that the ordinance was not properly tailored to prevent fraud, protect privacy, or reduce annoyance. He conceded that exercises of "pure First Amendment freedoms" deserved protection and were worth any inconvenience caused. Regulating advocacy combined with solicitation, however, had to remain within the power of municipalities chiefly becomes the "traditional" remedies suggested by the respondent are in fact unrealistic. To buttress this, Siegel introduced a small parade of horribles, suggesting that paid solicitors frequently ignored "no soliciting" signs and that trespassing complaints were too difficult to file under Illinois law.[75]

---

[74] Though the example was brought up somewhat suddenly at the end of the argument, the Girl Scouts would have made an excellent practical example with which to challenge both sides. While Siegel was quite eager to list them among the groups that would be eagerly welcomed into Schaumburg, the cost of cookies might be a sticking point. On the other hand, the Girl Scouts—one of the co-signers of the Coalition's *amicus* brief—would have tested the boundaries of Shadur's argument as well. In answering the Court's hypothetical's, Shadur had been willing to extend solicitation rights to individuals such as the college-bound youth, but would have revoked that right when the boy began selling magazine subscriptions to pay for college. Without adopting some version of Yarmolinsky's reasoning, it is not clear how Shadur would have defended the Girl Scouts' right to solicit.

[75] Siegel's exact wording contained a certain latent misogyny, suggesting that "unfortunately, bewildered housewives—and I don't mean to paint a horrible picture here—but it's a terrible burden on an individual housewife to have to go through the procedures, in Illinois at least, to file a complaint for trespassing" (Oyez *Schaumburg*).

McLain et al. v. Real Estate Board of New Orleans et al.

Throughout the twentieth century, politics in Louisiana acquired a certain reputation. Popularized by Robert Penn Warren's *All the King's Men*, the concept of corruption in the Bayou state was alive and well in the 1970s. Edwin Edwards was serving his first of four terms as governor. Roughly thirty years later he would begin serving a federal prison sentence for what many would consider the fitting end to a life filled with scandals of one kind or another. While corruption may be common in politics, the very publicness of it in Louisiana is the most striking thing. Running for his fourth term in 1991 against the equally unsavory David Duke, the popular rallying cries for Edwards' campaign were "Vote For the Crook. It's Important" and "Better a lizard than a wizard." (Poundstone 2008, 18)[76]

Politics, of course, is simply one venue for corruption. On November 6, 1979 the Supreme Court heard afternoon arguments in the case of *McLain v. Real Estate Board of New Orleans*. At issue was the question of whether realtors in the New Orleans area had engaged in collusion regarding price fixing of real estate brokerage commissions. Compared to the two cases above, the dynamics of *McLain* were fairly straightforward. Petitioners filed suit on federal anti-trust grounds, but essentially lost in the district court and in the Fifth Circuit Court of Appeals when it was held that they failed to establish that brokers' activities had a sufficient enough nexus with interstate commerce to implicate federal jurisdiction. The case itself never technically went to trial, having been dismissed after discovery. When the case came before the Supreme Court, then, several issues were at stake: the proper standard for holding that certain economic activity implicated interstate commerce, the status of the factual record in the lower courts, and the question of whether the lower courts had erred in dismissing the case based on their interpretation of available precedents.

The case for James McLain and the other petitioners[77] was argued by Richard Vinet. On a purely objective basis, Vinet was the least experienced attorney in the case. A graduate of Loyola University law

---

[76] In a somewhat ironic twist Edwards' second wife, Candy, has and does work as a real estate agent in Louisiana. Given that she was 15 at the time *McLain* was litigated, however, this fact is unrelated to the case at hand.

[77] While the case went forward in McLain's name and that of the Real Estate Board of New Orleans, it became a class action suit on both the petitioner's and respondent's sides.

school who had not clerked for a justice, Vinet only argued one case before the Court. Unlike some attorneys, he also left a fairly sparse trail. Over the course of his career he appears to have become an Assistant U.S. Attorney, as well as an attorney and Assistant Chief Counsel in the Department of Homeland Security.

Vinet began his argument with a standard summary of the case. Though he was able to make a fairly long opening statement, the Court interrupted quickly in order to seek clarification of Vinet's principal contentions. In fact, by my count, the first sixteen questions Vinet was asked had the attorney clarifying his description of what had transpired in the case, the petitioner's reason for filing for certiorari, the relevant language from controlling precedent, and how the petitioner's would hope to see the case resolved.[78] This might not be surprising, given that the Court was hearing *McLain* as a case that had never been fully tried. Even though the "real" question was one of applicable federal jurisdiction, the Court had to largely concern itself with whether the two courts below erred in their handling of the case. Throughout his time before the bench, Vinet was eventually able to make a few basic points: that the District Court had applied an erroneous interpretation of the *Goldfarb* precedent,[79] had prevented petitioners from discovering evidence that would have shown sufficient federal nexus, and therefore had prematurely ruled against McLain based upon insufficient evidence. Along the way, Vinet tried to pad his argument with relevant facts about how important real estate brokers are to the local economy, as well as to the interstate flow of money in the housing market.

---

[78] To count questions, I use the standard set forth in Johnson 2004 appendix 1. On that basis, Vinet was asked a total of thirty-two questions. The Court did not ask him a true hypothetical question until halfway through their colloquy. Even then, another twelve questions sought clarification in one way or another.

[79] *Goldfarb v. Virginia State Bar* (421 U.S. 773) had been decided four terms prior to *McLain*, and contained very similar situations. In the prior case, a husband and wife brought suit against the state bar, alleging that the minimum-fee schedule mandated for title lawyers constitute price fixing. The Court agreed, refusing to grant the bar any of a number of exemptions they had sought, and held that the mandatory use of a title lawyer to complete a title examination to receive title insurance, combined with the flow of interstate mortgage money, brought the bar association under the purview of the Sherman Act. One of the chief issues that Vinet covered in his time before the Supreme Court concerned the differences between title lawyers and real estate brokers—the chief one being that while brokers handle a good majority of transactions, their use was not mandatory as in the case of title lawyers.

The most awkward moment in Vinet's argument came shortly after a back-and-forth over whether the Court of Appeals opinion included any reference to petitioner's claims of limited discovery and whether brokers' price-fixing affected federal jurisdiction. Struggling a bit to address the Court's questions, Vinet accidentally referred to Justice Stewart as Justice Brennan. While Vinet seemed to recover fairly quickly and Stewart made light of the blunder, the incident was characteristic of an argument that never really gained momentum. Vinet faced some aggressive, though not truly hostile questioning. Justice Rehnquist, in particular, ended Vinet's time by forcing him to distinguish between claiming that the Court of Appeals and District Court had applied the wrong test versus claiming that two lower courts had made adverse findings of facts that petitioner objected to. On the other hand, he also received some very helpful questions—such as the one about how lowered commissions would lead to lower housing prices and what effect they would have on the mortgage market.

Vinet's adequate but not spectacular argument was followed by Frank H. Easterbrook, Deputy Solicitor General, arguing for the United States as *amicus* on behalf of McLain and the other petitioners.[80] As seems to be typical of those in the Solicitor General's office, Easterbrook stood at the opposite end of the experience spectrum from the counsel on whose side he argued. Only a year younger than Vinet, Easterbrook had been a undergraduate at Swarthmore and was a graduate of the elite University of Chicago Law School. While he did not clerk for a member of the Supreme Court, he had clerked for Levin Campbell on the First Circuit Court. A year out of law school he entered the Solicitor General's office as an assistant, making his way up to Deputy Solicitor General. By the time he appeared before the Court in *McLain*, Easterbrook had already argued in fifteen separate cases.[81] After his time in the administration, Easterbrook taught (and continues to teach) at the University of Chicago Law School. In 1995 he was appointed by President Reagan to the Court of Appeals for the Seventh Circuit, and

---

[80] The United States was one of ultimately three *amici* in the case. The National Association of Realtors filed a brief urging that the lower court ruling be affirmed. The Consumers' Union of United States, Inc. also sought to participate and successfully petitioned the Court; though their brief does not mention it, presumably respondents withheld their permission.

[81] After leaving the SG's office, Easterbrook made few additional appearances before the Court. As of 2009, he stood at nineteen lifetime arguments.

became Chief Judge of the same in 2006. At times, his name has been floated as a potential Supreme Court nominee.

Reading the transcript of Easterbrook's argument after reading Vinet's almost presents a difference between night and day. Where petitioner's counsel occasionally bobbled the answers to questions, Easterbrook consistently gave substantial, confident answers. Where Vinet found himself returning to questions he thought he had already answered, Easterbrook was able to answer questions and use almost every one to forward his claims. Where Vinet had his perhaps understandable gaff with Justice Stewart's name, Easterbrook seems to casually and easily weave the justices' names into his responses.

What is most striking, though, is the difference between the depth of evidence provided by the two attorneys. While Vinet was admittedly on the defensive a great deal of the time, addressing factual or quasi-factual questions about the case, he offered little by way of precedent to support his claims. He mentioned in passing, without discussion, *Mandeville Island Farms v. American Crystal Sugar Company* (1948) and *United States v. Yellow Cab Company et al.* (1947).[82] *Goldfarb v. Virginia State Bar* was repeatedly addressed, but never discussed in any detail. Vinet's argument rested entirely on factual descriptions of the importance of brokerages to local and interstate commerce, as well as a repeated claim that the lower courts had erred in their application of *Goldfarb*—although Vinet did little to support his own interpretation of that precedent. In contrast, Easterbrook personally led the Court on a tour of six specific cases and implicated other precedents.[83] Along the way various justices were at times skeptical, questioning him about the holdings and applicability of the cases. Easterbrook was able, though, to link them together into a multifaceted explanation for why the Court of Appeals' behavior had been so egregious in *McLain.*[84]

---

[82] 334 U.S. 219 and 332 U.S. 218, respectively.

[83] In discussing the difference between anti-trust and other cases, Easterbrook refers to "the gun cases."

[84] Throughout his argument, Easterbrook gives the impression that due to his preparation for argument, he would be nearly impossible to surprise. From comments about his demeanor in the courtroom as a member of the Seventh Circuit, Easterbrook appears to expect the same level of preparation from attorneys that argue before him. According to students he has taught, Easterbrook has made comments about longing to have a special button to push in order to open a trapdoor beneath unprepared counsel. Interestingly, the two flaws that

Respondents in the case were represented by Harry McCall, Jr., a Louisiana native who had risen to prominence in the local community. After graduating from Princeton, he attended Tulane Law School, and then began work at the firm of Chaffe, McCall, Phillips, Toler and Sarpy—the oldest established firm in New Orleans, where his father Harry McCall, Sr. had started work in 1915. McCall's charitable work was voluminous; he served on boards for the New Orleans Sewage and Water Department, New Orleans Children's Hospital, New Orleans Athletic Club, the Red Cross, and the Boy Scouts, to name only a few. He served as president of the New Orleans Bar Association, filled several roles at Tulane University Medical Center, had been secretary of the Louisiana Bar Association, and president of the Princeton Alumni Association of New Orleans. The list of his appearances before the Supreme Court is much shorter, but still marks him as above average. All told he would argue three cases before the Court. His first two were both in the 1979 term, arguing on October 1 in the case of *Vaughn v. Vermillion Corporation* (444 U.S. 206), and then on November 6 in *McClain*.[85]

McCall had, in a sense, an advantage in the *McClain* arguments. Vinet and his *amicus* had already argued, and Vinet neither reserved a portion of his time nor was allotted time for a rebuttal. That meant respondent's counsel would have the final word in the case, and could freely respond to all the opposing side's claims. Perhaps more importantly, he had the advantage of hearing the types of questions and concerns that the justices raised with the other attorneys. He began there, selecting as his first point a line of questioning that Rehnquist had pursued with Vinet. Contrary to what they may have claimed, McCall held that the case did boil down to petitioner's dissatisfaction with the lower court's adverse factual findings. McCall, however, went even further in faulting his opponents. The District Court gave McLain exactly the discovery that had been asked for—the opportunity to show *Goldfarb's*

---

seem to particularly raise his ire are failing to make a clear reason for why the court has jurisdiction, and showing ignorance of the trial record (Marek 2006).

[85] Excluding cases where multiple docket numbers were consolidated into one argument, McCall was one of 26 attorneys arguing multiple cases in the 1979 term. The majority of those (18) were attorneys for the federal government, generally from the Office of the Solicitor General. Five of the 26 were from a state attorney's general office or other lower-than-federal government entity. McCall, therefore, was one of only three private attorneys to argue more than one case in 1979.

applicability. No where in the record had they complained that their discovery had been limited in any way. In addition, petitioners had been demonstrably tardy in their discovery, failing to take any depositions until December, when discovery had been authorized in September and the deadline extended in October.

Perhaps McCall would have been fine had he concluded his point there. Instead he drew the analogy between petitioner's complaints about discovery and a hypothetical situation where a judge gave improper jury instructions but the litigant failed to formally lodge a complaint. Justice Stevens was the first to assault the analogy, forcing McCall to admit that there actually had been no trial in the instant case. Now on the defensive, McCall continued to lose ground. The bench claimed that the District Court's resolution of the case through a motion to dismiss supported by affidavits should be considered like a motion for summary judgment. That court, however, handled the dismissal in a way that contravened customary behavior—making no findings of fact before a judge with cross-examination, and ruling in such a way that either declared there to be no factual dispute or which presumed the version of facts least favorable to the losing party. Justices Rehnquist and White joined in the interrogation about the case's resolution. With a fair amount of chagrin, McCall had to ultimately concede his claims about the factual issues in the case.

Attempting to save face, McCall resorted to what he called his "second line of defense." While his first point was a procedural one, his second involved the claim that substantively, petitioners had been unable to show that the brokerage activity in the case had any substantial effect on interstate commerce. Unfortunately for McCall, the Court had just as many problems with his second defense. His own framing of the question trapped him when he said "However, then the question becomes: Have they shown, or can the evidence in anyway be construed or resolved to show a substantial effect on interstate commerce?" (Oyez *McLain*) Before McCall could elaborate, the Court immediately offered him a version of the same hypothetical that the other attorneys had received: what would happen to home prices if brokers raised their rate to 50 percent. His answer to the hypothetical left the Court wanting, as suggested by their repeated attempts to get him to give a clear answer. McCall reluctantly agreed that a 50 percent rate might affect prices, but resisted making the same claim about six percent, trying to mollify the Court by noting that the rate was actually a sliding scale and that the full six percent was charged only on the first $100,000 of the sale price.

Chief Justice Burger changed course slightly by asking McCall what the total value of real estate commissions was in New Orleans for a single year. McCall admitted he had no figure to offer, but strenuously resisted the Chief's suggestion, based on a comparison to numbers in the District of Columbia, that commissions could be in the millions of dollars. Telling McCall to presume a figure of $5 million, Burger restated the Court's question about whether the attorney believed that such a figure did or did not have an effect on housing prices. McCall took the interesting tack of saying that there is a possibility there could be some effect, but that he did not believe it—and that there was no evidence of it. Once again McCall tried to distract the Court by arguing that while housing prices in New Orleans had gone up a great deal, the level of real estate commissions had not. The Court did not bite and pointed out that commissions had in fact gone up because the total cost of homes went up. McCall retreated, asking the Court rhetorically for the proof that commissions had any effect on prices. To his vexation, this returned McCall to questions about why he held that a 50 percent commission would have an effect on prices but a six percent commission would not. When Justice Stewart phrased the question in the bluntest terms, "wouldn't there necessarily be an effect on the price of housing if you had free competition by contrast with a price-fixed commission", McCall's exasperation is almost palpable even in the written word alone: "Have I not answered that, Mr. Justice Stewart?"[86]

McCall's argument ended on a stronger note. Friendlier questions pointed out that the matter hinged entirely on whether interstate commerce was implicated, and that the question boiled down to whether the interstate mortgage money market and interstate home sales were affected. Counsel stated that the record was devoid of proof on those points. He further argued that real estate brokers were clearly engaged in intrastate commerce alone and that whatever effects there might be on interstate commerce were only incidental. For the first time in his argument, McCall turned to several precedents to support his contentions. Countering Easterbrook's use of the *Mandeville Island* case,

---

[86] If you view McCall's argument as a whole, the real conclusion of this line of questioning comes from Justice White, who united the impact of various commission rates with issues of the trial court's behavior, asking "what should a trial judge do, for anti-trust purposes, when he's making a—when he's going to resolve that at the beginning of a case? Should he resolve that in your favor or the other side's favor?"

McCall urged that the real controlling precedents on affectation doctrine[87] were earlier cases: the 1914 Shreveport Rate Cases,[88] *Apex Hosiery Company v. Leader* (1940), and the two Coronado Coal cases.[89] The Court asked McCall several questions about whether the situations in those cases were entirely analogous to *McLain*, but did not press their objections.

Lessons to be Learned

Three cases are far too few to draw valid conclusions about the 1979 term as a whole, let alone a broad range of terms. Nonetheless, some interesting comparisons can be had. That all three of the cases studied had liberal resolutions appears accidental. In *Mobil*, the Court ruled six to one that Vermont's tax did not violate either the due process or commerce clause provisions of the Constitution—an anti-business resolution to the case that was, arguably, "liberal" in nature although it benefited state power.[90] The outcome in *Schaumburg* was also liberal, with eight justices supporting Citizens for a Better Environment against the village's claims of police power. An eight justice Court was unanimous in *McLain*, supporting the petitioner, vacating the judgment of the Court of Appeals, and remanding the case for further proceedings. For comparison, approximately 53 percent of all cases in Gibson's database were resolved liberally, and liberal outcomes constitute 56 percent of all cases with oral *amici*. Looking at 1979 alone, a little over 46 percent of all the cases had liberal outcomes, and 47 percent with oral *amici* were so decided.

Switching from ideology to disposition, the petitioner's side prevailed in only one case, *McLain*. Across the board, cases are decided in petitioner's favor approximately 65 percent of the time. The percentage of wins by petitioners in cases with oral *amici* is slightly higher, at 68

---

[87] Affectation doctrine refers to the Court's rulings on how to interpret which actions as having the necessary impact, or affect, on commerce to bring it within the purview of federal law.

[88] *Houston, East and West Texas Railway Company v. United States* and *Texas and Pacific Railway Company v. United States.*

[89] *United Mine Workers of America v. Coronado Coal Company* (1922), and *Coronado Coal Company v. United Mine Workers of America* (1925)

[90] For purposes of description, I make use of the literature's standard definitions of "liberal" and "conservative." More information on the coding of these outcomes can be found in Gibson 1997, 72–74.

percent. In 1979 petitioners won 61 percent of all cases, but only 47 percent of cases with oral *amici.*

A more interesting story appears if one takes account of whose side oral *amici* appear on. Since 1979 only featured cases with solo oral *amici*, the math is fairly simple. Of the nineteen cases in the October 1979 term, thirteen appeared on behalf of the respondent. Across all of Gibson's terms, 329 cases had at least one more oral *amicus* appearing on one side or the other.[91] A full 210 of those had an imbalance for the petitioner and 119 had an imbalance for respondent. By this standard, the 1979 term was a bit unusual, with a higher than normal proportion of oral *amici* representing respondents.

When petitioners have the oral *amicus* advantage, they win approximately 77 percent of cases. Petitioners win only 43 percent of the time when respondents have the advantage. For the 1979 term, petitioners won 83 percent of cases with the advantage, and only 31 percent without it. This translates, on the whole, to an apparently large benefit to having oral *amici* on one's side. For all cases, the side most supported by oral *amici* wins 72 percent of the time. This figure is slightly higher, 74 percent, for the 1979 term alone. In *Mobil*, *Schaumburg*, and *McLain*, the side supported by an oral *amicus* won each time.

Such statistics offer no explanation for two outstanding questions: why oral *amici* are so influential, and how they ultimately come to participate in the cases that they do. This chapter's quantitative material has tried to approach these questions obliquely. To explain what oral *amici* provide and thus why they are influential, my hypotheses suggest a focus on information. To explain where *amici* appear, my results point toward certain factors that describe an information-poor environment. These answers, however, are only superficially satisfying. Truly understanding the influence of oral *amici* requires some clearer indication of their impact on decision makers—the kind of evidence that the *amicus* literature over all has had a difficult time generating. And to ultimately understand why oral *amici* appear in some cases but not others would demand access to the motivations for the many actors that control their presence: what drives an *amicus* to join a case in the first place, and what makes them seek to share argument time; what causes a litigant to either recruit oral amici, agree to share time with them, or

[91] To be complete, 384 cases in Gibson feature oral *amici*; once one excludes *amici* whose direction cannot be gauged, as well as cases where each side has the same number of oral *amici*, one is left with 329 cases.

deny them permission to participate at argument; and what drives the justices to grant or deny motions to share time for arguments.

Perhaps the most important, albeit also self-evident, point that arises from reading argument transcripts is that attorneys themselves are very important. While the literature reviewed in this chapter lays down more than enough anecdotal evidence on the subject, especially related to the prior experience attorneys bring to the Court, the contrast between strong and weak argument can be very striking. Of the nine appearances before the Court described above, the vast majority were average at best.[92]

In *Mobil*, counsel for the petitioners and for the respondents were, roughly speaking, evenly matched; while Hellerstein attended an elite school, neither had argued before the Court prior. Both had somewhat rocky arguments. Hellerstein brought the Court a novel argument about taxation which he was unable to offer much precedent to support. Several justices tried to push him to think through the implications of his arguments, such as the role of the interstate commerce clause. In the end, looking at Blackmun's rationale in the majority opinion, Hellerstein was his own worst enemy—failing to elaborate his due process claim and resting almost entirely on the idea that foreign source income was special, despite offering little evidence for the point. Arguing for Vermont, King fared about the same. Throughout his argument he struggled with the Court's hypotheticals, trying to duck some questions. After struggling, though, he was able to end with a few strong points focused on the weakness of Mobil's claims.

The attorneys in *Schaumburg* were also on an equal footing; both had argued a prior case, and both had attended the University of Chicago. Siegel's argument on behalf of the village, though, was clearly the rougher time. While tough questioning can be hard to interpret (c.f. Johnson et al 2009), throughout his time Siegel seemed to receive a fair amount of cynicism. The Court seems openly skeptical when it asks Siegel to defend the 75/25 split in expenses. The thin justification for the standard was matched by the limited connection he was able to draw between the ordinance's provisions and the triple goals of protecting citizens, protecting privacy, and preventing fraud. Shadur faired somewhat better for the CBE. While he was hounded by requests for a precedent that would support a First Amendment protection of solicita-

---

[92] My characterizations of the attorney's arguments are, of course, my own subjective judgments and might not align with how others would read the case.

tion in and of itself, he found solid ground in his criticisms of the arbitrariness of Schaumburg's 75 percent standard. Reading between the lines, Shadur's biggest opponent was Rehnquist, who tried both in his questions and in his dissent, to protect the power of municipalities. Though it apparently was not enough to convince the justice, Shadur's emphasis on the role of fraud and trespassing ordinances allowed him to avoid being backed into a corner.

McLain's argument was hard on both parties' attorneys. Despite the fact that the case turned so heavily on procedural details, Vinet found himself unable to move beyond them. At least part of the blame should be placed on his failure to marshal any real precedents to support his claims. With a prior argument to his name, McCall seemed to start his argument strong. Focusing on petitioner's reliance on *Goldfarb* and their failures at discovery, though, lead McCall into the unenviable position of defending the District Court judge. At several points he was either awkwardly forced to concede the Court's point in the face of repeated questioning, or awkwardly refused to agree to what the Court thought were self-evident facts. While Vinet may have confused the names of two justices, McCall's note of frustration reads as almost equally uncomfortable.

On the other hand, in each of the cases the counsel for *amici* fared much better. In arguing *Mobil*, Dexter brought with him two prior argument's worth of experience and the claim of being an expert on multistate taxation. Given his familiarity with three-factor apportionment formulas, he did come in for tough questioning about details of the method. The harshest criticism, though, seemed to come only from Justice Stevens whose dissenting opinion was well foreshadowed by oral argument. Yarmolinsky, arguing in *Schaumburg*, had not previously appeared before the Court. He was still able to make a very respectable showing. Even though the Court quickly moved away from the issues he began his introduction with, he rolled with the punches, addressing the Court's hypotheticals and conceding points where appropriate. And Easterbrook's argument in *McLain* was as close to perfect as one could imagine. None of the Court's questions phased him. More importantly, his argument was heavily laced with supporting precedent—something the other counsel lacked.

In his 1984 article on planned litigation, Stephen Wasby noted three reasons why *amici* might seek out a case: to reinforce a litigant's position by adding their voice to others, to reframe a party's case to better fit the *amicus'* needs or preferences, and to offer supplemental information or arguments that go beyond those of the party (Wasby 1984, 114). The three *amici* examined here clearly exhibit the third category. In each case, the amicus presented a broader view of the case, its impact, and the legal context. Dexter embedded Vermont's tax system in a broader, settled framework that emphasized the novelty of Mobil's desired outcome. Yarmolinsky transformed Shadur's limited claims about non-traditional charities into an across-the-board indictment of how Schaumburg's ordinance hurt all charities. Easterbrook transcended the details of a single jurisdictional dispute to demonstrate the connections between disparate lines of precedent. Given the limited nature of argument time, it is not surprising that *amici* spend little time providing simple "me too" reinforcement. On a more interesting note, there appeared to be little reframing going on. In *Schaumburg*, Yarmolinsky attempted to argue against the village's ordinance because a "patchwork" of ordinances would make life difficult for national charities. Aside from a minor clarification question, the Court spent no time on the alternate frame.

The idea of supplementing the parties makes even more sense in light of Songer et al.'s "Why the Haves Don't Always Come out Ahead" (2000). In that piece the authors investigated the "haves versus have-nots" logic made famous by Galanter 1974, but applied to state supreme court litigants. Most research had shown that one-shot litigants are almost always at a significant disadvantage compared to repeat players who appear in Court regularly.[93] The Songer et al. article found, much to their surprise, that one-shotters can effectively equalize their standing when more experienced *amici* join their side of the case (Songer et al. 2000, 553; c.f. Simmons 2009, 204).

Once oral arguments are taken into account, this *amicus*-supported equalization takes on a compound form. One part relates to the litigants and *amici* themselves. Even without analyzing detailed litigation histories, it is fairly easy to decide which of the parties represents the "least advantaged." Sheehan, Mishler, and Songer have offered a ten-point scale to categorize litigants based on relative resources, in which higher numbers represent greater resources and arguably a greater advantage

---

[93] Repeat players are generally any business, government institution, or group that stands in a position to appear in multiple court cases. The quintessential example is a landlord, who could likely appear in many landlord-tenant disputes. Since any given tenant is unlikely to ever be in more than one case, they are defined as "one-shotters."

ment time does end up getting shared in what could be seen as "low information environments." Attorneys are part of the equation. An overall lack of argument experience in front of the Court seems to correlate with oral *amici,* who tend to be more experienced on average than the counsel for the parties. An examination of three cases has shown how attorneys arguing on behalf of *amici* can present cases more clearly, lay a broader perspective for the case, and respond more directly to the kinds of questions the Court wants to explore. At least in the three cases considered here, these attorneys appeared to be successful; the cases were all decided in their favor, and the Court's opinion included a great deal of the logic they laid out during oral argument.

The results from this chapter, though, are clearly just a first step. There are at least five improvements that need to be made. The most basic improvement would be to create a larger dataset, inclusive of more Court terms. With more data, a controlled regression analysis would make it possible to see how the impact of inexperienced attorneys compares to that of other factors that might be at play. In addition, expanded data would allow for the testing of more specific hypotheses about when oral *amici* might appear on a particular side in a case. Similarly, a broader pool of cases will mean more opportunities for detailed case studies. Given that each of the cases discussed in this chapter resulted in a win for the side supported by the oral *amicus*, a possible selection bias might have resulted in conclusions that are not broadly true for other cases.

Second, my models include only a subset of the characteristics often included in discussions of attorney quality. While prior argument experience is the only trait that proved significant in my own models, a fuller picture of attorneys would also include whether each individual was a previous member of the Solicitor General's office, a law professor, or a member of the so-called "Washington bar" of highly experienced appellate attorneys.[95] Third, the impact of government attorneys needs to be more properly controlled for. While the Solicitor General and other members of the office have more experience on average, there might be insight to be gained from separating out what happens

[95] Some evidence does exist that not all these traits do in fact relate to attorney quality or experience. See Johnson et al. 2007.

in the courts (Sheehan et al. 1992; c.f. Collins 2004). Using this syste the petitioners in *McLain* would be categorized as a 3 (individuals) a the respondents as either a 4, 5 or 6 (unions/interest groups, small bu nesses, or businesses respectively). *Schaumburg* would be scored as 8 versus a 4 (local government against an interest group). The *Mo* case represents a bit of a challenge. On a technical basis, Mobil wo be categorized as a 7 (corporation), and the Vermont tax commissio as a 9 (state government). Practically speaking, though, the power multinational Mobil Oil Corporation might have a claim to greater sources and greater potential repeat-player status than Vermont.[94] I accept that premise, the *amici* in each of the three cases argued on side of the most resource-disadvantaged litigant.

Comparative resource standing is only one part of the equati however. Supplementing the parties can also mean supplementing th attorneys with higher quality argument. As one former Assistant to Solicitor General was quoted above, the Court looks for effective pr entations—which in part means direct answers to questions (Bri mann 2003, 69). The three cases examined here do not all feature *a cus* counsel that are more experienced than their litigant counterpa But one thing this chapter shows is that experience—and its presum consequence, "quality" argumentation—is hard to quantify objective Subjectively speaking, on paper the three *amicus* counsel were m poised, less rattled by confrontation with the justices, and more dir or concise with their answers to the Court. Their presence in each ca might not have been the decisive factor that swung the Court in th direction, but the winning parties definitely seem to have benefitt from the support of their *amicus curiae* and from the argument by *a cus* counsel.

CONCLUSION

Judicial scholars have known for some time that the *amicus curiae* is important part of the Supreme Court's litigation process. This chapt seeks to round out our knowledge of *amici* by examining their presen at oral argument in light of the Court's information needs. While m findings are only tentative and do not directly answer what orall arguing third parties do to meet those needs, it appears clear that arg

---

[94] For a different take on situations where businesses might have the advanta over certain government entities, see Wheeler et al. 1987, 439.

when government counsel appear, whether as counsel for a party or as an *amicus*.[96]

Fourth, a more discriminating analysis would differentiate between cases where oral *amici* are present by the leave of a party, versus cases where the *amicus* petitioned the Court in order to participate. Since the final decision about the presence of *amici* is made by different groups in each instance, there might very well be some difference between the types of cases. The general principle that oral *amici* fulfill the Court's information needs should hold either way—though it might be that the justices themselves gauge their need by a different set of factors than the ones that parties use. Examining the orders from cases in the 1979 term, *amici* sought the Court's permission to participate in ten cases. In only two cases did the Court grant the motion, both of those being petitions from the Solicitor General's office.[97] Given the extreme paucity of such cases, it seems reasonable to treat oral *amici* as a group until a larger dataset is obtained.

Finally, a focus on information needs alone might not properly encompass all explanatory factors. At least in theory, one can imagine that the litigants' general level of economic and social resources, and in particular the presence of a disparity between the two sides, could serve as a type of catalyst. Oral *amici* might be more likely to appear when one party faces an additional deficiency in its resources. In other words an individual citizen as party to a case against a corporation or the government, where the individual's attorneys have comparatively less experience before the Court, might attract oral *amici* in a way that other cases might not. In such instances, an attorney's experience is more

---

[96] The literature is not entirely clear on what to expect from this kind of separated analysis. A good case has been made in McGuire 1998 that the high success rate for the Solicitor General and other government attorneys might simply be the result of far more time arguing in the Court. Nonetheless, there is still evidence that points to the personal success of the SG when presenting as oral *amicus* (Segal 1988, 140). In addition, Pacelle 2006 at least offers the possibility that different types of appearances by government counsel (e.g. invited versus not, as party versus as *amicus*) could reveal differing impacts on the Court.

[97] Having made only two petitions to the Court for leave to participate in argument, the Solicitor General's office had a perfect track record during the term. None of the Court's eight denials were to organs or functionaries of the federal government, except for *Harris, Secretary of Health, Education, and Welfare v. McRae et al.* (448 U.S. 297), concerning state funding for abortions under Medicaid. House Majority Leader Jim Wright had sought to participate in oral argument, but was denied by the Court.

than just a potential way to inform the Court—it represents a component of the broader discussion of fairness and justice in the litigation process. Given that the qualitative case studies in this chapter point to a dynamic of litigative "haves versus have-nots," the effect deserves exploration at the quantitative level as well.

An *amicus curiae* at oral argument is in many ways an oddity. The Court disfavors them, and parties are hesitant about sharing their time with them. And at least on some understandings of how the justices make their decisions, their presence should largely be irrelevant. The next chapter examines whether oral *amici* do in fact have any impact on the Court, looking at case votes and written opinions.

CHAPTER 3

Influence on Case Outcomes

The previous chapter suggested that the appearance of oral *amici* is not an entirely random phenomenon—that certain conditions make it more or less likely for them to be present. One important factor is information. Attorneys serve as conduits for information. While this happens in the briefs they file, this function takes on even greater importance in their appearances before the Court. During oral arguments, justices explore untouched policy questions and begin to form coalitions with other members of the Court (Johnson 2004, 126). It appears that in instances where the parties' attorneys have an overall lack of experience, counsel for *amici* may serve as something of an antidote, increasing the Court's potential for gathering information by offering additional experience or greater quality.

This observation means very little, though, if the Court pays no attention to this information. In this chapter I examine whether the presence of oral *amici* has an impact on the actual decisions that the Supreme Court makes. This investigation will take three forms. First, I will develop a model that identifies whether parties with greater oral *amicus* support experience greater success in case outcomes. Second, I examine how oral *amici* affect the actual votes cast by members of the Court. Finally, I will look beyond the dispositions of cases to see how the claims made by *amici* at oral argument affect the substantive policy holdings in Court opinions.

THE VOTE ON THE MERITS

As described in Chapter 1, it has proven extremely difficult to find conclusive evidence of the impact of third party *amicus curiae* briefs. The problem arises in part because of behavioral equivalence. There are so many competing forces that can influence the Court, and not all of them can be clearly distinguished from each other in the data. For example, when the Court rules in favor of a party, on its face it can be difficult to say whether they did so because of the party or because of the party's *amicus*.

Two factors control the ability to make that distinction. First is the choice of where to look for results, and the second is the choice of what instrument to use in order to uniquely identify the contribution made by *amici*. The first, crudest level at which one could attempt to discern the impact of oral *amici* would be on the simple binary outcome of a case—whether litigants are more likely to win when they have extra oral advocates on their side. Tests of this kind focused on *amicus* briefs in general have been discouraging; selecting identical cases that differed only by virtue of *amicus* presence, Songer and Sheehan failed to find that such briefs made any difference in a case (Songer and Sheehan 1993).

Part of the difficulty is that research has found certain predictors to be extremely effective at identifying justices' votes and case outcomes. Policy preferences, in particular, have proven to have such great explanatory power that many scholars argue for reading the whole of judicial behavior through this lens. Discussing the question of whether respect for precedent has any limiting effect on the justices, one pair of scholars answers in the negative. To explain why precedent appears at all, they offer two possibilities: "[f]irst, because the need for legitimacy is real, the justices must cloak their policy preferences with legal doctrine.... Second, we must never underestimate the ability of humans to engage in motivated reasoning. For all we know, the justices actually believe that they resolve disputes by appropriate modes of legal analysis" (Segal and Spaeth 1996, 1075; c.f. Epstein, Landes, and Posner 2009, 3).

While defending or critiquing such presuppositions is generally beyond this work, it is clear that when examining the outcomes of cases, scholars cannot neglect the justices' preferences. To properly trace the impact of oral *amici* in and of themselves, therefore, all efforts must be made to find an instrument that captures only the influence of third parties themselves. The path to participation in oral arguments as described in the first chapter suggests at least one possible pitfall. On its face, it is impossible to tell whether an oral *amicus* is present because the parties have given their consent or because the members of the Court have granted the group's motion to appear. In both instances, the fact that the group makes it to argument would likely still be important. When the Court is responsible for their presence, though, it is possible that the justices' policy preferences could explain what groups appear and therefore what their likely contribution will be to the case. As with precedent, oral *amici* could simply be a cloak of legitimacy thrown over the Court's existing choices.

Table 3.1: How *Amici* Gained Permission to Participate in Oral Arguments (1953–1985)

Who Granted Permission	Number of Amici	Percent
Litigant Permission/ SG Volition	270	74.38*
Court Permission	93	25.62
Total	363	100

The difference between these two categories is significant, $p < .001$

One quick way to answer this concern is to take the set of cases featuring oral *amici* and examine the orders issued in each case. When the Court explicitly gives a group "leave to participate in oral argument as *amicus curiae*" or grants a motion for divided argument filed by an *amicus*, it seems reasonable to consider the case potentially tainted by the justices' preferences. In all other cases, where the orders leave no record of oral *amici*, the parties themselves are the instigating force.[98] The oral *amici* in such cases are the best vehicle to use when comparing the explanatory power of *amici* versus that of preferences. Examining all the cases covered in Gibson 1997, namely the 1953–1985 terms, shows that most oral *amici* arrive by the effort of the parties (see Table 3.1).[99]

Given confidence that a substantial majority of *oral amici* can be separated from the Court's influence, I can use this group of cases to probe the comparative influence of oral *amici* against and controlling

[98] The same principle can be extended to instances where the Solicitor General appears at oral argument. When the SG is invited by the Court, hidden policy preferences may be a complicating factor. In other cases where the SG chooses to participate, there is less cause to worry.

[99] This data was gathered using Lexis.

for other explanations of the Court's behavior. This influence, I believe, will be noticeable at both the individual and aggregative level. That is to say, oral *amici* will noticeably impact both how each justice votes—controlling for the powerful influence of policy preferences—as well as how cases are ultimately decided. This suggests the following two hypotheses:

> ***Case Outcome Hypothesis*** **($H_{3.1}$).** The presence of *amici curiae* at oral arguments will have a direct and significant effect on the outcome of cases decided by the Supreme Court.

> ***Justice Vote Hypothesis*** **($H_{3.2}$).** The presence of *amici curiae* at oral arguments will have a direct and significant effect on the votes cast by members of the Supreme Court.

Data and Methods

To test these hypotheses I estimate two separate sets of models, relying on Gibson's *United States Supreme Court Database, Phase II: 1953–1985* (1997). Going beyond the features found in Spaeth's database, Gibson includes details about the individual *amici* in each case, such as the position taken, the number of co-signers on the brief, and whether the *amicus* appeared at oral argument. From Gibson I selected all cases that were fully argued and came to the Court by way of certiorari or direct appeal. This constitutes a population of 4635 cases measured by docket number, stretching over the courts of Chief Justices Warren, Burger, and Rehnquist.[100]

---

[100] This number could be somewhat larger, but several cases were excluded for technical reasons. Four cases were listed in Gibson's data without a docket number. Another 199 cases whose issue area was coded as "miscellaneous" were excluded to better match the types of cases considered in previous studies. Because judicial ideology serves as one of my variables, I eliminated 46 cases where the disposition did not have a clear ideological direction. For a similar reason, 1688 specific observations were dropped because the votes of specific justices could not be determined. Finally, I chose to exclude *Brown v. Board of Education* (1954). Given the sheer number of *amici* in the case and the particular circumstances, it seems reasonable to treat it as an anomaly from the Court's normal procedures.

Aggregate Model: Dependent Variable

To determine whether the presence of oral *amici* affects case outcomes, my aggregate dependent variable is whether the Supreme Court reversed (coded as 1) or affirmed (coded as 0) the lower court's decision. I use this variable in three separate rare events logit models: one which includes all cases in the sample, one which focuses only on civil liberties cases, and a third focused on economics cases. By estimating separate models in this fashion, I can find the overall impact of oral *amici*, as well as how they perform in subcategories of cases where preferences are known to be especially effective, in varying degrees (c.f. Segal et al. 1995).

Aggregate Model: Independent Variables

Amici, as a general phenomenon, can influence the Court in several ways. To account for the potentially separate influences of *amici* submitting briefs apart from those who appear at argument, I include a variable that captures the former. Since the dependent variable in this model is based upon case outcome, I measure the presence of *amici* as the number of briefs supporting the petitioner minus those for the respondent. This variable ranges from 33 more groups supporting the petitioner to 37 more groups against the petitioner. The mean value of the variable is .02, and has a standard deviation of 1.823.

Research has shown that judicial ideology can alter the Court's propensity to affirm or reverse lower cases (Palmer 1982; Boucher and Segal 1995). To compensate, I include a variable that takes on the value of 1 when the Court median and the lower court decision do not match ideologies (e.g. one is liberal but the other is conservative, and vice versa).[101] This variable is coded as 0 when the two ideologies match, reflecting the presumed likelihood that the Court will affirm the lower decision.

I include several other standard controls that may reflect differences in how the justices decide cases under differing circumstances. To capture the possibility that the impact of *amici* may be shaped by the influence of the sitting Chief Justice, I include a variable that is coded 1 for all cases decided prior to the 1969 term (Warren), and 0 for

---

[101] The median is based on the percent of liberal votes cast by each justice in each of Spaeth's (2001) twelve issue areas for all years prior to the current term. From there I aligned the justices for each term within each issue area and determined the median. If the median voted liberally more than 50 percent of the time he was considered liberal.

all cases after (Burger and Rehnquist). The Court's reaction to the potential ramifications of a case is captured using the method described in Maltzman et al. 2000, in which declarations of constitutional infirmity or formal overturning of precedents are coded as 1. To capture the public visibility of a case, I use a dummy variable that indicates whether an account of the case appeared on the *New York Times* front page (Epstein and Segal 2000).[102] As in the previous chapter, I measure the legal complexity of a case based on whether it involved multiple legal provisions or not.

My independent variable of interest concerns the presence of oral *amici*. Similar to my control variable for *amicus* briefs, I measure this as the number of oral *amici* supporting the petitioner minus those who support the respondent. This variable ranges from two to negative two, with a mean of .02 and a standard deviation of .273. I expect this variable to be significant and its coefficient positive, suggesting that even controlling for other forces the presence of oral *amici* urging reversal increases the probability that the Court will do so (and vice versa). As explained above, I only include *amici* that have been allowed by the parties.[103]

Justice-Level Model: Dependent Variable

The best test of the influence of oral *amici* would be to examine the situation that best maximizes known explanatory forces; in other

---

[102] This measure is frequently referred to in the literature as political salience. I prefer to avoid this term because it requires making an assumption about the basis on which a case might be important. Actually, two presumptions are required. First, one makes an assumption about the group to whom the case is important. Second, one makes an assumption about the point at which that decision is rendered. The Epstein and Segal measure, for example, presumes importance based on the newspaper reading public and the journalists that choose which cases make the list. It is also a measure that is available after a case has been decided.

The measure from Maltzman et al. is also often referred to as legal salience. As with political salience, I believe this term to be flawed. Almost by definition, any case that the Court handles is automatically salient in a legal sense. I use the term ramifications to reflect on the fact that cases where the Court overturns itself or bases its decision on constitutional judicial review represent something of an extraordinary circumstance whose effects are potentially farther reaching than that of a case in which neither happens.

[103] When the model was estimated ***only*** on the cases where the Court granted permission for an *amicus* to appear, the results do not change—except that there is no statistical significance in civil liberties cases.

words, to truly test oral *amici* I need to look not just at the case level, but at the justice-case level, where ideology is so particularly effective. In the second set of models designed to test the Justice Vote Hypothesis, the dependent variable is the justice's vote in a case. By switching to this level of analysis, I have a dataset of 39,790 total individual case-votes. This dichotomous variable is coded based on the ideological direction of the vote, following the convention that 1 represents a liberal vote.[104] This model will also be estimated for all cases, just civil liberties cases, and just economics cases.

Justice-Level Model: Independent Variables

When examining justices' votes, a full suite of control variables is called for. First, I include a measure of *amicus* brief filings; given that this model features an ideological dependent variable, I code *amici* based on their ideological direction instead of the outcome they argue for. Also included are the other case-level variables from the aggregate model.

To measure the political preferences of the Court's justices, I make use of the measure developed by Martin and Quinn (2002). While the idea that ideology guides judges stretches back decades, measuring those preferences has been difficult. The newspaper-based scores developed in Segal and Cover 1989 were a huge advance over endogenous measures. Martin/Quinn scores, however, have the advantage of reflecting longitudinal changes in an individual justice's ideology (c.f. Epstein et al. 1998; Martin and Quinn 2002). They are also more effective across a variety of issue areas than are Segal/Cover scores. The most liberal justice in the dataset measures at –6.71, while the most conservative scores a 4.39. The overall mean ideology is –.193, with a standard deviation of 2.256. This variable should be both statistically significant and negatively signed, such that an increasingly liberal (i.e. negative) ideology score will likelihood that a justice will vote liberally.

[104] C.f. Gibson 1997, 72–4 and Epstein et al. 1996, 485.

Table 3.2: Rare Events Logit Model Estimating the Effect of Oral *Amici* on the Court's Decision to Reverse a Case

INDEPENDENT VARIABLE	*ALL CASES* COEF. (ROBUST SE)	*CIVIL LIBERTIES* COEF. (ROBUST SE)	*ECONOMICS* COEF. (ROBUST SE)
# of More Oral Amici for Reversal†	0.634 (.134)***	0.535 (.178)**	0.519 (.270)
# of More Amicus Briefs for Reversal†	0.090 (.019)***	0.100 (.029)***	0.149 (.040)***
Likelihood of Reversal	0.796 (.064)***	0.541 (.093)***	1.188 (.124)***
Warren Court	–0.135 (.065)*	–0.153 (.096)	–0.073 (.124)
Case Ramifications	0.223 (.108)*	0.078 (.122)	1.256 (.370)***
Case Visibility	0.047 (.086)	0.132 (.107)	–0.293 (.180)
Multiple Legal Provisions	–0.136 (.078)	–0.409 (.100)***	0.062 (.162)
CONSTANT	0.228 (.056)***	0.435 (.078)***	–0.048 (.108)
MODEL SUMMARY			
Number of Observations	4635	2399	1354

* $p \leq .05$ (one-tailed test) ** $p \leq .01$ (one-tailed test) *** $p \leq .001$ (one-tailed test)

† These variables are measured as how many more *amici* there are urging reversal compared to affirmance.

In the justice-level models, my measure of oral *amicus* participation indicates how many more liberal than conservative *amici* were present at oral arguments. This was coded from Gibson's variables indicating which side the *amicus* supported and the ideological direction of the Court's decision. This variable has a mean value of .014 and ranges from negative two (two more conservative than liberal groups) to two (two more liberal than conservative group). I expect this variable to be statistically significant and signed positively.[105]

Results

Results for the three aggregate models can be found in Table 3.2. Even with other explanations available, there appears to be confirmation for the Case Outcome Hypothesis. While the Court's decision does seem to be influenced by the overall presence of *amici*, and while a Court inclined to reverse appears to do so (in most cases), the further appearance of third parties at oral argument affects the Court with a noticeable significance ($p < .01$).[106] On their own, these models do not entirely answer the question of why or how oral *amici* make the difference that they do. As described in the first chapter, allowing a third party to ap-

---

[105] My reasoning here parallels Collins' findings regarding an ideological imbalance of *amici* altering justices voting patterns (Collins 2008, 112–114).

[106] Both the aggregate and justice-level models were run with an additional variable, an interaction term to capture the possible connection between the oral argument variable and the ideological variables (likelihood of reversal in the case-level model, individual Martin/Quinn scores in the justice-level model). In only one model did the interaction term even approach statistical significance: the economic submodel at the justice-level. However, because the significance of an interaction term can sometimes be disguised by multicollinearity among independent variables, I also ran correlations for the interaction variables and their components. In the justice-level model, the variables correlate very poorly (less than 0.1).

In the case-level data, the correlation between the interaction term and the oral argument variables is actually quite high—0.760, to be precise. This sug-gests that the interaction term could in fact be significant, but simply masked by the other variables. Given that it is difficult to determine which is the case, I also ran predicted probabilities for the model including the interaction term. In no instance did the added presence of the interaction variable significantly alter the results; in general, most numbers were simply altered by a few percent.

Given these minimal changes and the ambiguity in knowing if the interaction term is significant, I report the model without the interaction term.

pear at oral arguments may serve as a signal from the litigant to the Court. Because this signal rises above the level of cheap talk, the justices are predisposed to respect it. Alternately, the impact of oral *amici* might be less about the signal that their presence represents. Chapter two pointed toward the idea that oral *amici* provide the Court with information that may be particularly persuasive or helpful.

Table 3.3: Predicted Probabilities that an Imbalance of Oral *Amici* alters the Court's Propensity to Reverse Lower Courts

	+2 *AMICI* FOR RESPONDENT	BASELINE	+2 *AMICI* FOR PETITIONER
All Cases	.439	.739	.909
Civ. Liberties	.481	.729	.886
Economics	.652	.757	.900

* All variables are held at their mean or mode. Numbers in the table are derived by ranging variables between the smallest and largest values in the sample.

Logit estimates are best interpreted in a predictive context. To that end, I used the ReLogit software described in King and Zeng 1999, which takes the results of a rare events logit model, combined with hypothetical values for independent variables, to translate coefficients into a probability for the dependent variable given the specified conditions. The probabilities for the aggregate models can be found in Table 3.3 and depicted in Figure 3.1. In the model that includes all cases regardless of issue area, the baseline probability of reversal is 74 percent. This number is calculated by setting all the variables to their mean or modal value. Holding all other variables in the model constant, the impact of oral *amici* is clear when I range the variable from its minimum to maximum values. The presence of two more *amici* arguing for reversal at oral argument increases the chance of reversal to 91 percent. This drops to 44 percent when two more *amici* argue for affirmance instead. When focusing solely on economics and civil liberties cases, the probabilities are similar. Reversal probabilities for civil liberties cases vary between 48 and 89 percent. The range is 65 to 90 percent for economics cases.

Figure 3.1: Predicted Probabilities of Reversal that an Imbalance of Oral *Amici* alters the Court's Propensity to Reverse Lower Courts

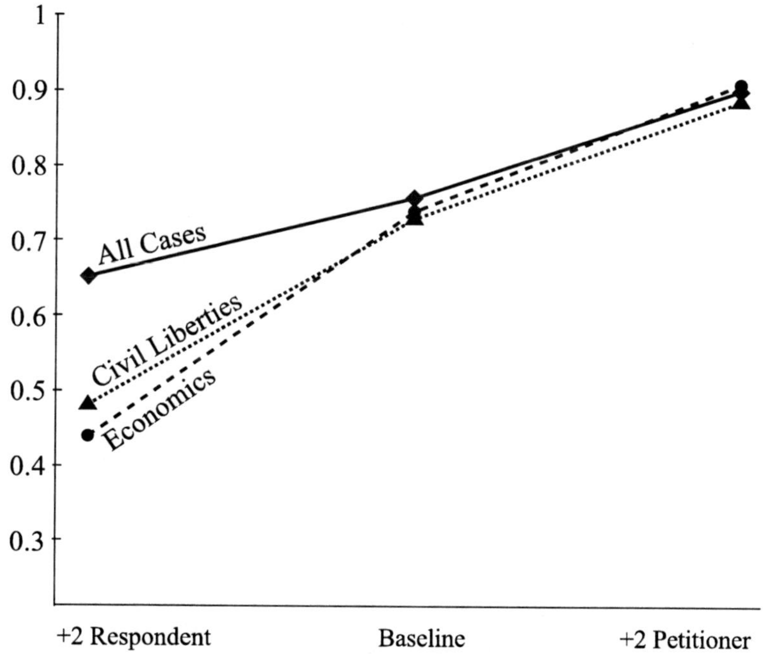

Even more dramatic evidence for the importance of oral *amici* comes from the models that estimate individual justices' votes, found in Table 3.4. As expected, personal political ideology does affect how a justice votes; the negative coefficient indicates that as the numerical value of ideology increase (representing more conservative beliefs), the propensity to vote liberally decreases. But even controlling for ideology, the justices still react to oral *amici*. When more liberal groups appear at argument than do conservative ones, the result is a statistically significant ($p < .001$) liberal shift in all justices' votes. Since this effect is separate from that of groups simply filing *amicus* briefs, these results strongly reinforce research that argues for the impact oral arguments have on the justices' own decisions (c.f. Johnson 2001; Johnson 2004). Even when only looking at civil liberties cases or economics cases, oral arguments are still significant.

Table 3.4: Rare Event Logit Model Estimating the Effect of Oral *Amici* on the Liberalness of Justices' Votes

INDEPENDENT VARIABLE	*ALL CASES* COEF. (ROBUST SE)	*CIVIL LIBERTIES* COEF. (ROBUST SE)	*ECONOMICS* COEF. (ROBUST SE)
# of More Liberal Oral Amici†	0.572 (.042)***	0.475 (.064)***	0.552 (.086)***
# of More Liberal Amicus Briefs†	0.062 (.006)***	0.079 (.011)***	0.089 (.013)***
Ideology	–0.294 (.006)***	–0.465 (.010)***	–0.182 (.010)***
Warren Court	0.399 (0.022)***	0.391 (.033)***	0.338 (.040)***
Case Ramifications	0.965 (.040)***	1.376 (.050)***	–0.620 (.095)***
Case Visibility	0.154 (.029)***	0.124 (.038)**	0.033 (.062)
Multiple Legal Provisions	–0.064 (.026)*	–0.427 (.036)***	0.304 (.057)***
CONSTANT	–0.138 (.016)***	–0.083 (.023)***	0.223 (.032)***

MODEL SUMMARY			
Number of Observations	39,790	20,726	11,483

* $p \leq .05$ (one-tailed test) ** $p \leq .01$ (one-tailed test) *** $p \leq .001$ (one-tailed test)

† These variables are measured as how many more *amici* there are urging a liberal outcome compared to a conservative outcome.

Table 3.5 presents the predicted probabilities for the justice-level model, based on King and Zeng's program. In these results, the dependent variable is the likelihood that a given justice will cast a liberal vote in a case. To show the true impact of oral *amici*, this table demonstrates two types of changes. First, it indicates the effect of varying the number of oral *amici* between the minimum and maximum values. Second, since the principal challenger for explaining votes is ideology, I break down the results for three hypothetical justices: one whose ideology is that of the median justice, one who is the most liberal member of the Court, and finally the most conservative justice. This information is also shown in Figure 3.2.

Table 3.5: Predicted Probabilities that an Imbalance of Oral *Amici* makes Individual Justices' Dispositive Votes More Liberal

CONDITIONS*	+2 CONS. *AMICI*	BASELINE	+2 LIB. *AMICI*
ALL CASES			
Most Cons. Justice	.071	.194	.430
Moderate Justice	.228	.481	.745
Most Liberal Justice	.668	.863	.952
CIVIL LIBERTIES			
Most Cons. Justice	.045	.107	.237
Moderate Justice	.281	.503	.724
Most Liberal Justice	.890	.954	.982
ECONOMICS			
Most Cons. Justice	.243	.358	.629
Moderate Justice	.425	.562	.795
Most Liberal Justice	.707	.807	.926

* Predicted probabilities are for the most conservative justice in the dataset (Martin/Quinn = 4.39), a moderate justice (M/Q = –.193), and the most liberal (M/Q = –6.71). All other variables are held at their mean/mode; baseline reflects no imbalance of *amici* in either direction.

Figure 3.2: Predicted Probabilities that a Given Justice will Cast a Liberal Vote, Based on Presence of Oral *Amici*

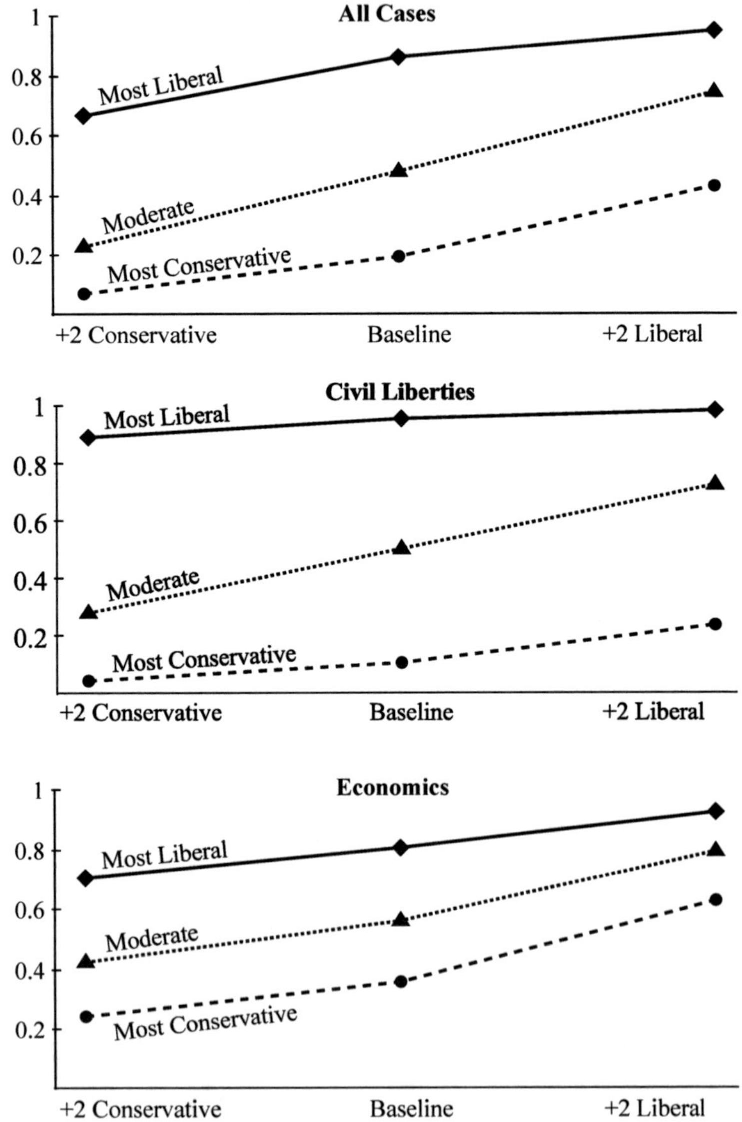

Several important things are clear from these predicted probabilities. First, the justices' ideology is still an important explanation for how they vote. Across all the issue areas, conservative and liberal justices maintain distinct propensities to vote their ideology. At the same time, third parties at oral arguments are also influential. Paralleling the findings in Collins 2008 about *amicus* briefs overall, all justices—regardless of the issue—find themselves pulled in a conservative direction when there are more conservative oral *amici*, and pulled in a liberal direction when the balance favors liberal *amici*. The extent of this pull does vary by issue. In civil liberties cases, where ideology is known to be strongest, the lines for conservative and liberal justices are both at their farthest from each other and are also flatter; while oral *amici* affect such cases, they do so to a lesser degree. *Amicus*-based voting changes for liberal justices are only 9 percent, and the change is 19 percent for conservatives. This is compared to a 28 and 36 percent change when all cases are included. On the other hand, the situation is different for economics cases. Conservative and liberal justices are closer to each over all and the size of the impact made by oral arguments is also a bit larger: 39 percent for the most conservative justice and 22 for the most liberal.

By far the most interesting results concern the justice with a median ideological score. Across the three specific models, the impact of oral *amici* on that justice is constant, even in civil liberties cases, where the difference is on the order of a 44 percent change in propensity to vote liberally. Conservative and liberal justices, though clearly influenced by oral *amici*, are still likely to vote conservatively or liberally. [107] Not so for the moderate justice. In all of the situations examined, moving from more conservative to more liberal oral *amici* entirely switches the moderate justice's voting tendencies.[108] This is not an insignificant finding. For decades, appointments to the Supreme Court have become battlegrounds because of the perception that changing the

[107] This is certainly true for the model that includes all cases and for the civil liberties model. Referring to the graph of the results from the economics model, the liberal end of the conservative line and the conservative end of the liberal line both hover near or at 50 percent.

[108] Given the appearance that moderate justices are especially influenced by oral *amici*, I explicitly tested for interaction effects using quadratic measures of ideology, absolute values of ideology, and a series of ideology dummy variables. Since none of these measures was significant, I believe that the model as presented here is a satisfactory specification.

Court's ideological makeup can change the Court's policy.[109] When a Court is split nearly evenly, and one moderate justice stands in the middle as a swing vote, the real outcome of the case—both in terms of disposition as well as policy content—may be decided by how many oral *amici* appear in the case.

ORAL AMICI AND COURT OPINIONS

The first chapter of this book outlined various ways that scholars have tried to discern the impact of the *amicus curiae.* Most of those methods have been inconclusive. I am confident the results presented above have demonstrated that, at least when it comes to oral arguments, *amici* can affect case outcomes. However, the causes and extent of that effect are still unknown. One way to explore this *amicus* effect would be to look beyond case disposition to the policy holdings the Court lays out in its majority opinion. While every case has a simple binary outcome, the legal arguments that the Court accepts or rejects in the course of its opinion are both less predictable and arguably more important. The case's disposition settles the immediate dispute, but the holdings in the case carry the precedential weight that shapes cases yet to come.

In chapter five of his book *Oral Arguments and Decision Making on the United States Supreme Court,* Johnson tries to answer a similar set of questions about oral arguments broadly considered. For Johnson, solid evidence for the value or arguments would be found if it could be shown that a significant portion of the Court's holdings arose from the arguments themselves and not from another source, such as the parties' briefs. To test his hypotheses, Johnson analyzes a sample of seventy-five cases. For each, he identifies the arguments made in the majority opinion's syllabi and then seeks out whether those arguments appeared in the litigants' briefs and whether they were addressed during the Court's questioning at oral arguments. In cases with the participation of *amici,* Johnson also separates out whether the arguments appeared in an *amicus* brief (Johnson 2004, 96).

---

109 Given the predictive power of ideology, there is truth to this contention. Of course, justices can change their ideology over time, justices may act with restraint despite their ideology (e.g. Kennedy in abortion cases), and the Court's power to effect true policy change is circumscribed by other actors. Nevertheless, it is the appearance of criticalness that is most important here.

This approach is not without its drawbacks.[110] It does, however, represent perhaps the best and most accepted method for conducting this analysis. It also yields promising results. Johnson finds that of the forty-five cases without *amicus* participation, forty-four percent of syllabus points were found in briefs as well as in the Court's questions at oral argument (Johnson 2004, 99). More importantly, a full third of syllabus points were touched on in oral argument alone. In comparison, only eleven percent of syllabus points had a sole origin in briefs, while twelve percent appeared to have no discernable source.

Johnson also offers his findings for the thirty cases in his sample that have *amicus* participation. Though adding *amicus* briefs as an additional source for syllabus point does compound the number of sources arguments can come from, his results still suggest the importance of oral arguments. Fifty-two percent of syllabus points could be traced to oral arguments and some combination of litigant brief, *amicus* brief, or both. Another twenty-four percent of points had no origin other than what the Court asks attorneys during oral argument. Compared to non-amicus cases, a slightly higher percentage of syllabus points came from briefs alone—eighteen percent. Only six percent of syllabus points lacked a matching reference in cases with *amicus* participation (Johnson 2004, 99).

Data from Cases with Oral *Amici*

Johnson's work strongly suggests that oral arguments are an important and frequently independent source for the information included in Court opinions. It seems logical, therefore, to adopt a similar approach to show the value of oral *amici curiae*. As an initial study, I select a

---

[110] Difficulties fall into at least three categories. On the one hand, this method requires a somewhat difficult cross-source content analysis whose subjectivity may be unpredictable. Further, this method might not fully reflect how often the justices refer to oral arguments in their opinions. In a note, Johnson acknowledges that syllabi are written by court reporters, which introduces the influence of a separate party into the equation. Many references to what transpires at argument may not find their way into the shortened summaries contained in a syllabus (Johnson 2004, 153n1). Finally, even though the Court might adopt points advanced by *amici*, there is not easy way to be certain that the points are not serving as a post hoc justification for the Court's actions (Collins 2008, 34).

Table 3.6: Origin of Information in Supreme Court Majority Opinions with *Amici* at Oral Argument

WHERE INFORMATION ORIGINATES	NUMBER OF REFERENCES	
Briefs Alone		**11.11%**
Party brief only	0	0%
Amicus brief only	2	3.70%
Party and *Amicus* brief	4	7.41%
Oral Argument Alone		**0%**
Party argument only	0	0%
Amicus argument only	0	0%
Party and *Amicus* argument	0	0%
Briefs and Oral Argument		**83.34%**
Party brief + Party arg.	3	5.56%
Party brief + *Amicus* arg.	1	1.85%
Party brief + Party arg. + *Amicus* arg.	1	1.85%
Amicus brief + Party arg.	1	1.85%
Amicus brief + *Amicus* arg.	0	0%
Amicus brief + Party arg. + *Amicus* arg.	5	9.26%
Party brief + *Amicus* brief + Party arg.	14	25.93%
Party brief + *Amicus* brief + *Amicus* arg.	3	5.56%
Party brief + *Amicus* brief + Party arg. + *Amicus* arg.	17	31.48%
No matching reference	**3**	**5.56%**
Total Issues in Syllabi	**54**	**100%**

random sample of twelve cases from the Burger court era.[111] Following Johnson, I code each syllabus point from the majority opinion and then

[111] My sample is technically drawn from all orally-argued cases, with *amicus* participation at oral argument, issued with full decisions from the 1980 term to the end of Burger's time on the Court. I time-limit the population in this manner to ensure ease of Court argument transcripts and written briefs.

determine if the point was raised during questioning at oral argument, in written briefs, or both. To meet my goal of demonstrating the relevance of oral *amici*, I increase Johnson's information sources by one to include whether a syllabus point was touched upon in the questioning of parties versus that of the oral *amicus*. While Johnson must ultimately account for eight possible information source combinations, my addition leaves me with sixteen possible combinations. My sample of sixteen cases contained 54 total syllabus points, for an average of 4.5 points per case. Johnson's data contained 4.16 points per case overall, with 4.27 in cases without *amici* and 4 points in cases with *amicus* briefs. The results of my analysis can be found in Table 3.6 and a comparison with Johnson's results is depicted in Figure 3.3 and Figure 3.4.[112]

To lay a basis for comparisons, a few things should be said about Johnson's findings. Notable differences appear between cases with and without *amicus* participation. When any *amici* are present in a case, the number of syllabus points that lack a clear source drops from 12 percent to 6 percent—quite logical, given the vital information function that third party briefs provide. This drop is accompanied by a similar drop in the percentage of syllabus points drawn from oral argument alone. While the justices' opportunity to question attorneys during argument is still important, at least some of their information gathering needs seem to be met by the additional written resources. Aggregating together the different types of briefs shows that they serve as an exclusive information source for 18 percent of syllabus points; this number is up from 11 percent in cases without *amici*. Across the board, though, oral arguments are demonstrably important. Even with a drop in the number of points taken from argument alone, there is essentially no change in the number of points that are at least touched on in argument (77 compared to 76 percent).

Purposely including cases where *amici* appear at oral argument allows for an even more refined look at the Court's information sources. One thing that appears is a decreased reliance on solo information sources. As shown in Table 3.6, in the 12 cases and 54 syllabus points

---

[112] Detailed results from Table 3.6 have been aggregated into Johnson's eight categories for comparison. Numbers have been rounded to the nearest whole percent. Figure 3.4 separates-out those categories from Figure 3.3 based on whether the syllabus point was found in the brief of the *amicus* that presented oral argument, some other *amicus* brief, or both.

analyzed from oral *amicus* cases, a little over 11 percent of points were drawn from briefs alone and no points were drawn solely from the Court's argument sessions. While this latter point might seem surprising given all that has been said about the value of oral argument, it may be explainable in two ways. First, it might be the result of having a limited sample of only twelve cases. Second, the apparent decrease in the use of oral argument could simply reflect the increased number of briefs filed in such cases. The mean number of *amici* in the 4635 cases quantitatively analyzed in the first half of this chapter was 1.48, while the mean for the twelve cases considered here was 5.25. It is certainly plausible that with so many written sources of information, there is a much lower chance that the justices will use oral argument to introduce into the case some previously undiscussed issue.

As with Johnson's data, the modal category was that which included the most information sources. Thirty-one percent of all syllabus points could be described as being ones that were widely discussed, appearing in both litigant and *amicus* briefs as well as the oral argument of the litigants and *amicus*. Second only were syllabus points raised in both types of briefs and discussed in the questioning of the litigants, at 26 percent. Similarly briefed points that occurred only in *amicus* argument constituted just 6 percent of the total. While this might suggest that the oral argument of the parties seems to be a richer information source than does that of *amici*, it should be noted that if one looks at cases where points were raised in just one type of brief, slightly more points were raised by *amici* and then discussed in oral argument (11.71 percent) than were points raised only in litigant briefs and then discussed in argument (9.26 percent).

Figure 3.3: Comparison between Johnson's Information Sources and those in Cases with Oral Amici

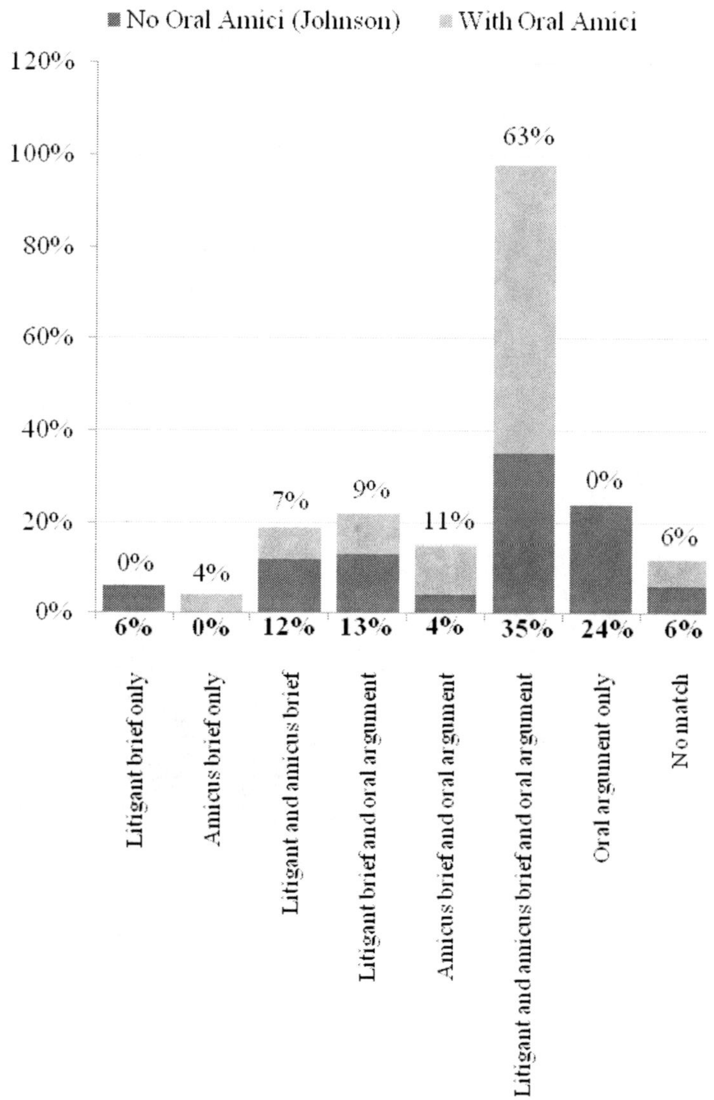

Figure 3.4: Comparison between Johnson's Information Sources and those in Cases with Oral Amici

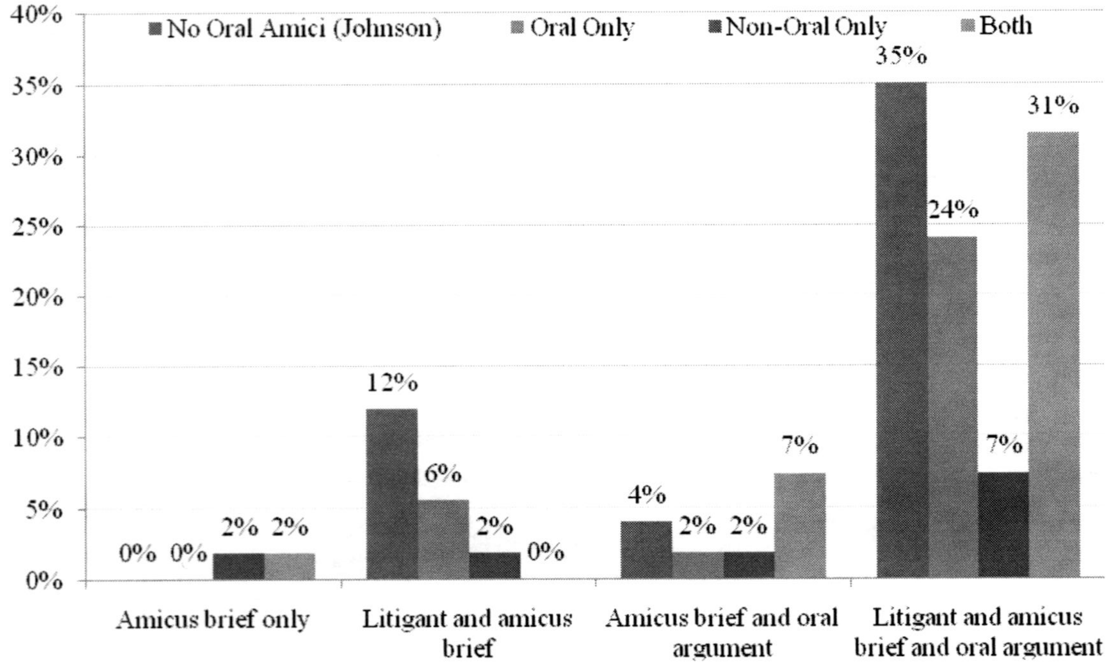

In Figure 3.3 I provide a side-by-side comparison of the information sources for cases with *amicus* briefs and those with *amici* at argument. To best allow for comparison, I have collapsed the categories from Table 3.6, consolidating third party and litigant arguments. Categories without *amicus* briefs all show decreases, while the categories of *amicus* brief alone and *amicus* briefs with argument show increases. This reflects, I believe, the increased importance of *amicus* contributions in these cases. As discussed above, the data also show a noticeable drop in points drawn from argument alone. This is matched, though, by a nearly two-fold increase in the number of syllabus points that can be traced back to litigant briefs, *amicus* briefs, and oral argument combined. The percentage of the Court's holdings drawn from *amicus* briefs and argument also increases, from four to eleven percent.[113]

One important question that these aggregate numbers do not answer is whether the *amici* that these points are drawn from are the same that appear at oral argument. Figure 3.4 helps address this point by highlighting those categories from Figure 3.3 that include *amicus* briefs. In this second figure, the first bar indicates Johnson's original data; the second bar represents the percentage of points drawn from the brief of the *amicus* that appears at argument, the third bar those *amici* that do not appear, and the fourth bar those points that can be traced to both types of briefs.

One thing that appears from this breakdown is that the briefs filed by non-oral *amici* play only a minor role in the Court's opinions—at least when considered in isolation from the oral *amicus*. Only thirteen percent of syllabus points come from such sources, with more than half of those also found in litigant briefs and oral argument. While the oral *amici* do not appear noticeably more prominent when examining syllabus points drawn from briefs alone or *amicus* briefs and argument, nearly a quarter of all points can be traced to the combination of the brief of the oral *amicus*, the litigant's brief, and argument. The dominant category, however, appears to be points that get mentioned in the

[113] While in a way it would be gratifying if most of these points were ones raised in *amicus* briefs and then in the argument with *amicus*, Table 3.6 shows that not to be true in the sample of twelve cases. That the vast majority of these points, though, are raised by the *amicus* brief and are then found in both sets of arguments is perhaps more important.

briefs of both oral and non-oral *amici*. When those figures are added to the others, roughly 72 percent of syllabus points are somehow touched on by the briefs of oral *amici*, either alone or in conjunction with non-oral briefs. By contrast, only 53 percent of syllabus points are touched on by non-oral briefs. The former number is particularly interesting given that using a similar calculation, the number of points touched on by litigant briefs stands at 79 percent.

Discussion

While the sample here contains only twelve cases, I believe that it allows for some preliminary comments on whether oral *amici* impact the Court's policy outputs. Part of that discussion must include the visible tension between the role of *amici* and that of oral argument itself. As discussed in chapter two, the Court has a variety of ways to meet its information needs. Both the questioning at oral argument and the filing of briefs by *amici curiae* can serve this function. Comparing Johnson's sample of 75 cases with the twelve analyzed here shows that as one moves from cases without *amici* to cases with *amici*, and then cases with oral *amici*, arguments are less likely to be a solo source for the Court's syllabus points. What is not clear from this is why it happens. A quantitative increase in the number of *amici* in such cases might simply make it more likely that the Court will use points raised by third parties. As Figure 3.4 shows, though, when information sources are broken down to separate points drawn from the briefs of oral *amici* and those of the non-oral, it does not appear that a large percentage of points come from the latter. Many of the Court's points can be traced to both types of briefs, but oral *amici* appear to have the edge in terms of citation. These results reinforce the value of *amici* over all. More fundamentally they point towards the importance of understanding which *amici* appear at oral argument. Oral *amici* have an apparent double value, since the Court draws upon the questions asked of their counsel at argument and also draws more of its holdings from their briefs than from those of other *amici*.

At the same time that these results suggest the importance of *amici* themselves, nothing entirely diminishes the value of oral argument. Though no syllabus points can be traced exclusively to argument in the twelve cases considered, over 83 percent of points were touched on in argument in some fashion—more than in Johnson's cases that feature *amici*. Correspondingly, in cases with oral *amici* fewer points are drawn solely from the briefs that have been submitted. Whereas 18 percent of Johnson's syllabus points came from litigant and/or *amicus* briefs, only 11 percent of points do in oral *amicus* cases. Without doing a more detailed study that examines the content of the questions asked in oral *amicus* cases, it is difficult to say if the justices are using argument in exactly the same ways that Johnson describes. For example, in cases with oral *amici* the Court may spend less of its time using oral argument to solicit the preferences of external actors. Sixty-nine percent of syllabus points about external actors came from oral argument alone in Johnson's data (Johnson 2004, 106). In cases with greater numbers of *amici* and those where at least one *amicus* is allowed to present argument, it may simply be more common for those issues to occur both in some set of briefs as well as in the justices' questions.

Table 3.7: Number of Syllabus Points that can be traced to Oral *Amici* in the 1979 Supreme Court term

MENTIONED...	NUMBER OF POINTS	
In argument with oral *amicus*	27	50.0%
but not argument with the parties	4	7.4%
In the oral *amicus'* brief	39	72.2%
but not the briefs of the parties or other *amici*	2	3.7%
By oral *amicus* in any way	48	88.8%
but not by the parties or other *amici*	0	0.0%

Apart from detailing the relationship between *amici* and argument, the ultimate goal of this analysis was to determine if oral *amici* make an impact on the Court's policy. By most basic indicators, the answer is "yes." Considering the source of syllabus points, the relevance of oral *amici* could be demonstrated in several ways. The Court could cite holdings that were discussed with *amici* during argument. Oral *amici* could also be successful if the points from their briefs made their way to the Court's opinion.

Table 3.7 aggregates these results for 1979 cases. When friends of the court appear at argument, their material clearly gets incorporated into cases. No matter whether one looks at argument, briefs, or both, a majority of syllabus points can be traced to oral *amici.*[114] While it might be initially disappointing that few syllabus points have a solo origin with oral *amici*, it should not be read as undercutting the fundamental results. Given all the places the Court can receive information from, oral *amici* are unlikely to be responsible for more than a minority of the Court's holdings—otherwise one would expect to see more friends at argument than one actually does. Still, the Court appears to pay attention to what these friends do provide.

Given that most of the syllabus points traceable to oral *amici* can also be found in other sources, it is tempting to see this as an answer to the question of whether friends of the court should focus their efforts on adding new information to a case or simply reiterating material introduced by the parties.[115] While scholars and practitioners still puzzle over which is a more effective strategy, my immediate findings can offer no clear answer. Because the analysis in this chapter looks at the issue from the point of view of the majority opinion, I can be certain that the Court does enshrine into law repeated information. But without examining all the actual points made in *amicus* and litigant briefs, nothing definitive can be known about whether repeated information constitutes a majority or minority of what the briefs advocated. Knowing what percentage of a brief's points were repeated versus new information would then make it possible to know what percentage of each get cited.

Even with that type of investigation, though, certain methodological problems would linger. Working solely from entries in the case syllabus might still miss lines of reasoning that made their way from briefs into argument, but which did not appear in the case's resolution. I also maintain that the distinction between new or repeated information may be too simple and blunt to be useful. Not all "new" information ends up being relevant or useful for the justices. How information is received is almost certainly conditioned by a group's identity. A well known and respected *amicus* might be more "successful" when reemphasizing a party's claims, especially if the party is resource-disadvantaged compared to its opponent. On the other hand, a chorus of *amici*, each adding something new about a case's potential impact, might prove very

[114] Entries for oral *amicus* briefs in Table 3.7 are calculated as the number of points drawn exclusively from their briefs (but not those of non-oral *amici*), as well as points mentioned in both oral and non-oral *amicus* briefs.
[115] See the conversation on the matter in Chapter 1.

influential in the right circumstances.[116] Any further attempt to analyze this lingering debate about information types should certainly pay attention to the actual types and categories of claims put forward in a case (c.f. Johnson 2001, Johnson 2004).

CONCLUSION

This chapter has set out two principal findings. First, when *amici* are present at oral argument, they have a statistically significant impact on their case. Whether measured in the aggregate as case outcomes or at the level of individual justices' votes, the influence of oral *amici* remains even when controlling for other known factors. On the whole, the magnitude of this influence does not overwhelm other variables in the models. But in the right circumstances, such as a case where one moderate swing vote could change the outcome, the presence of friends at argument may mean the difference between victory and defeat.

The disposition of a case is only part of the equation. In his synoptic study of *amici*, Paul Collins observed that "the paramount goal of amicus participation is to employ legal persuasion to influence the outcome of the Court's decision as it relates to the policy announced in the case" (Collins 2008, 31). An examination of cases from the 1979 term suggests that oral *amici* are able to influence the policy holdings in majority opinions just as they impact the outcome of the case. The issues raised by *amici*, both in their briefs and those discussed during their time in the Court's chamber, are those that the Court enshrines in its opinion. While most of these points have also been raised by the parties and other *amici*, friends at oral argument are certainly not irrelevant for a case's outcome.

In the end, there are many more questions that need to be asked about how oral arguments affect the decisions made by Supreme Court justices, and more specifically about the role of *amici curiae* at these proceedings. One obvious next step for this research is to expand the analysis from the second half of the chapter to include a larger selection of terms. If, along the lines of Johnson 2001, these expanded data were to be accompanied by a categorization of the arguments from briefs, the questions asked during argument, and the points in opinion syllabi, I would be able to examine whether oral *amici* are asked different types

---

[116] One example might be that of the Puyallup cases described in Chapter 2, where the presence of multiple states' attorneys general might have shaped the Court's final position on treaty and fishing rights.

of questions and whether the information they provide the justices is of a noticeably different variety from that of the parties.

The fact that oral *amici* do influence both outcomes and policy points back toward the questions of Chapter 2. Who are oral *amici*? How do a particular set of friends end up at argument? Is there a specific way in which these groups impact the Court? An even more important question without an immediate answer is whether oral *amici* have the impact they do because they have been allowed to share argument time, or whether they are simply "superior *amici*." It may be that certain groups are more likely to appear at argument because of some exogenous factor related to quality: attorney experience, prior Court appearances, quality of legal argumentation, political or social stature, etc. This factor or combination of factors may be responsible for explaining the presence of *amici* at argument as well as their influence on the Court. Rather than being an effect of argument, what I have observed might simply be the result of the greater likelihood of success enjoyed by some *amici*.

My suspicions are that this is not the case. Appendix 1 and Appendix 2 list the *amici* that participated in oral argument between 1953 and 1985. The federal government is clearly responsible for a large number of appearances. This opens the possibility that the Solicitor General's impact as a third party at argument simply mirrors its success in other arenas. Apart from that, the fact that the list of oral friends is as diverse as it is—including subnational governments, high profile groups, but also many low profile groups—makes it difficult to discern any factor that might *prima facie* point to an *amicus'* superiority.

There is also the possibility that *amici*, when they appear at argument, are a procedural fluke that has little to do with the case's outcome.[117] Issues asked of *amici* during questioning do appear in Court opinions. But rather than provide some novel information about or per-

---

[117] This need not be read as suggesting that oral *amici* are irrelevant entirely. One could imagine third parties gaining access to argument time for symbolic reasons. This would, in effect, be indistinguishable from the type of "window dressing" argument that a follower of the attitudinal model might advance. Instead of serving to cloak the justices' true motivations in making decisions, though, the presence of oral *amici* might simply fulfill a different set of goals. For example, a litigant might choose to allow a group to share argument as the result of a personal favor or the desire to further relations between the groups in the future. For a broader discussion, see Epstein, Landes, and Posner 2009 or Simmons 2009.

spective on a case, *amici* might get cited simply because they are present. Rather than waste the time of a group that has made its way through the procedural barriers to participation, the Court might engage *amicus* counsel in a colloquy about issues that would become holdings anyway. The interesting part of the story might not be what *amici* offer the Court, but simply what conditions make it likely that the parties or justices will allow them to be present. A satisfying answer to this challenge requires further data, along the lines of the issue categorization mentioned above. If oral *amici* are asked a different category of questions or a good portion of holdings drawn from *amici* are different from those of the parties, there would be support for my belief that the presence of oral *amici* is actually meaningful for decision making.

These are just some of the issues that need to be addressed in the next round of research on this subject. Nonetheless, I believe that there is enough evidence at hand to warrant further investigation. *Amici* may appear at argument in only a minority of cases, but their presence clearly leaves its mark.

CHAPTER 4

Conclusions and Implications

A REVIEW OF THE FINDINGS

Chapter one of this book began by telling the story of *Kennedy v. Louisiana* and how the Supreme Court ruled that the death penalty could not be imposed for the rape of a child. In the end, Texas Solicitor General Cruz's appearance as an oral *amicus* was unable to sway the Court in Louisiana's favor. This places *Kennedy* in the minority of cases, since across the board the side most supported by oral *amici* tends to win.[118] Of course, oral *amici* are not some miracle cure that inevitably leads to victory. Neither common sense nor any of the results of this project lead to that conclusion. I do believe, though, that some initial answers can be offered to the questions posed in chapter one about the importance of oral *amici*.

As a first investigation of this aspect of the Court's operations, my principal goal has been to explore what meaning can be ascribed to any *amicus curiae* that appear at oral argument, with an emphasis on two

---

[118] Using Gibson's dataset for 1953 through 1985, a total of 384 cases out of 4635 had oral *amici*. Of those, 320 cases had a single oral *amicus* clearly urging a specific case outcome. The side supported by the oral friend won in 233 cases, approximately seventy-three percent of the time. Cases with multiple oral *amici* are a bit harder to capture. Only seven cases had multiple oral *amici* with an imbalance for one side or the other. Four of those were decided in the favor of the side with the most oral support. For comparative reference, fifty-five cases in the dataset are coded as having an equal balance of oral *amici*. In those cases, forty cases—about seventy-three percent—were decided in the petitioner's favor.

ways that *amici* could be meaningful. The Information Provision Hypothesis I introduced in the first chapter was further developed in the second, where I examined the possibility that the presence of oral *amici* might be driven by the attorneys themselves. In a lecture given at the June 2004 meeting of the Supreme Court Historical Society, John Roberts—not yet Chief Justice of the Supreme Court—observed that attorneys presenting argument before the Court were akin to "medieval stonemasons" (Roberts 2005, 79). The goal of the analogy was to describe the laborious process of preparing for oral argument. For Roberts, researching the case, rehearsing answers to hypothetical questions, enduring mock court sessions are like the effort put into carving gargoyles on medieval cathedrals. Far removed from the public eye, both argument preparation and the elaborateness of the mason's carving are vital to their completed products.

Roberts' analogy is exceedingly *apropos*. Both cathedrals and Supreme Court cases are composites. Part of the final product boils down to raw ingredients, either the builder's stone or the legal questions and facts of the case. Equally important, though, is how those materials are worked by artisans. A skilled mason can take a humble stone and transform it into something transcendent. A skilled oral advocate illuminates the dynamics of the case, clarifies the issues involved, and tries to present their client's position in the most appealing and persuasive manner possible.

Not all attorneys, however, are equally skillful. As discussed in chapter two, the literature is replete with measures for how to grade, rate, and compare attorneys. Most of these rely upon the attorney's education and training. I focused on three such measures: whether the attorney attended an elite law school, whether they had clerked for a member of the Supreme Court, and their number of prior arguments. Of the three, the simpler measure of experience seems most important. The number of prior arguments an attorney has made before the Court serves as a direct benchmark of their level of skill. When both attorneys have limited experience, it is far more likely that their case will include an oral *amicus*.

These findings do not necessarily explain why greater experience before the Court should have any meaning beyond triggering the presence of oral *amici*. As detailed in chapter two, the side supported by friends at argument faces a much better chance of succeeding; conversely, the side without oral support is even less likely to win than it would otherwise. A host of potential explanations might arise for what might just be a confluence of events. Nonetheless, if attorney experience is a key, it seemed reasonable to examine the actual behavior of attorneys. I considered three cases from the 1979 term.

Based on this admittedly nonscientific sample I was able to draw a few conclusions. Some mistakes that attorneys make, while traumatic at the time, are fairly mundane. On occasion an attorney forgets a justice's name or calls one by the wrong name. Such moments are awkward, of course, but it is open for debate whether problems with names are more or less embarrassing than the examples of attorneys fainting during argument that Justice Roberts cites (Roberts 2005, 73). While even an experienced attorney can make an accidental mistake, it seems reasonable that greater experience before the Court leads to greater comfort with the actual proceedings. Greater comfort should in turn lead to fewer technical mistakes.

It would strain the bounds of believability, though, to suggest that verbal gaffes or stage fright are the deciding factors in a case. Whatever benefits accrue from experience—or from attorney quality, for which experience is a proxy—should be more consequential. The benefits should also be readily identifiable. Subjective evaluations of an attorney's performance are easy to make, but are just that: subjective. To say an attorney did "a better job" than another says little about what was actually done. The literature reviewed in chapter two offers some possible approaches for how to objectively evaluate performance and what "good" attorneys bring to a case. McGuire spoke of "credible advocacy" and its ability to reduce the complexity of information available (1998). Brinkmann, a former member of the Solicitor General's office who has personally argued before the Court, spoke of the importance of direct responses to the justices' questions (2003, 69). Chief Justice Roberts describes the same advice (2005, 73).[119]

Mobil Oil, Schaumburg, and McLain all offer examples of behaviors that reflect this logic. Attorneys who lost in these cases: pushed novel claims without providing what the Court appeared to believe was sufficient rationale; attempted to duck the Court's questions or bobbled hypotheticals; got trapped in procedural minutiae that failed to touch on the significant legal issues in their case; actively argued with the Court;

[119] Some research on attorney experience suggests that the influence of quality argumentation may be conditional on case circumstance. In particular, cases that are highly salient from a political or legal viewpoint appear to show less influence from attorneys (McAtee and McGuire 2007, 273).

and grudgingly backtracked on their claims when pressed heavily by the justices. Conversely, attorneys who fared better often did the opposite. Amicus counsel in these cases specifically provided broad, integrated explanations of the case and its importance. They offered and explained more precedents. They directly addressed the Court's questions, even when doing so led them away from their own argument. And when caught in contradiction or error, they gracefully conceded the point.

Having found that the presence of oral *amici* is not entirely random, the question became whether their presence is consequential. The Amicus Impact Hypothesis I proposed suggested that cases with oral *amici* would be more likely to be decided in the direction supported by the *amicus*. Chapter three elaborated on that suggestion. At the aggregate level, I hypothesized that the actual dispositions of cases would be skewed towards the side with oral *amicus* support. For cases where friends argued on both sides, the party with more oral *amici* was considered to have the advantage. Testing this hypothesis with a dataset of over four thousand cases orally-argued covering a span of thirty years, I found significant support. While other factors clearly play a role in determining the likelihood of a reversal—such as the Court's preexisting inclination to reverse, based on ideology and the direction of the lower court's decision—oral *amici* do make a difference. Based on the predicted probabilities found in Table 3.3, when there are enough oral *amici* supporting respondent, compared to petitioner, the chances that the Court will reverse the case actually drop below forty percent.

In addition to shaping the outcome of cases, I found that having friends at oral argument has a discernable impact on justices' individual votes.[120] Taking into account the ideological direction of an *amicus'* position allowed the influence of oral argument groups to be tested against other known factors. The results were very encouraging. In addition to being significant, pronounced imbalances of oral *amici* alter any justice's propensity to vote liberally. As with the results in Collins 2008, this influence is seen across the board. On average the shift

[120] Other research into oral argument has suggested that arguments may have an influence on justices regardless of their own specific behavior at argument (Epstein, Landes, and Posner 2009, 21). The chief evidence presented is the fact that Justice Thomas, while steadfastly refusing to ask questions in almost any case, still tends to vote against the party that received the harshest questioning.

amounts to some thirty percent. That number, though substantial enough, masks the fact that shifts in voting behavior are even larger for moderate justices. This is one of the most exciting discoveries, as it points toward the possibility that oral friends might occasionally be a deciding factor in a case's outcome.

In the second half of chapter three I used Johnson's methodology for determining if the effect of oral *amici* on dispositions could also be seen in the legal holdings that determine a case's policy impact. Taking this step is vital to understanding oral *amici*. An observed impact on whether a case was reversed or affirmed cannot explain the reason for the impact itself. It most certainly cannot confirm that *amici* play an informational role for the justices. For that I turn to the Court's holdings. Comparing the specific legal positions taken by the majority opinion to those advocated by the different parties or groups involved in a case makes it possible to draw conclusions about the relative influence of those involved.

A random sample of twelve cases from the Burger court paints a complicated picture of cases with oral *amici*. In none of the cases I examined did a syllabus point find its sole origin in oral argument. Across the board, actually, fewer points were drawn from "solo" sources than in the cases that Johnson examined (Johnson 2004, 99). This seems reasonable. Separately considering oral *amici* increases the possible information sources for the Court. Increasing that number also makes it more likely that information may come from multiple sources. Even with these caveats, the evidence is still positive about the value of oral arguments. Only a small percentage of the Court's holdings seem to be drawn from briefs without any connection to oral argument. By contrast, more than three-quarters of holdings have been discussed orally.

Within this lattice of overlapping information sources, the *amici* that head to oral argument fare well. Their relevance shows in two ways. First, about half the time the Court's holdings have been discussed not only at oral argument, but with *amicus* counsel at argument. This goes a long way to showing that when friends are present at argument, the issues discussed with them end up being relevant for the Court's opinion. The second point in their favor is the fact that items from oral *amicus* briefs are more likely to be sources for the Court's holdings than are the briefs of non-oral *amici*. All told, it seems safe to suggest that oral *amici* do seem to matter, not only in the disposition of cases but also in the actual legal policies they establish.

Improving the research

Almost no prior research has examined the role of oral *amici*. Collins' synoptic work on friends of the court almost purposely skips the topic (2008, 15). As such, there are many ways in which the work in this book can and needs to be expanded on. Chapter two, on the factors influencing the presence of oral *amici*, has room for improvement in three major areas.

First, even though most of the attorney quality variables proved insignificant, it may be that other measures of quality might be different. The literature on attorneys also points to past experience in the Solicitor General's office, time spent as a law professor, and membership in the District of Columbia "appellate bar" as possible factors. In addition, it might be interesting to specify an alternate model using Justice Blackmun's oral argument grades as a synoptic measure of attorney quality (c.f. Johnson, Spriggs, and Wahlbeck 2007). This approach might help counter the apparent minimal role for any specific attribute of attorney experience.

Of course, one of the biggest things that would improve my confidence about the attorney experience hypothesis would be a larger dataset. Collecting data for more than a single term would allow greater confidence overall and would reduce the possibility that results were affected by factors particular to a single term.[121] Additional data would also make it possible to introduce case-specific factors as controls, and more allow me to test more specific hypotheses than those laid out in the chapter. Attorney inexperience may trigger the presence of oral *amici*, for example, but is it the case that those *amici* generally appear on the side of the inexperienced counsel? It also may be that different factors shape whether *amici* appear for the petitioner versus the respondent.

Future research should also separate factors that are currently lumped together. At the moment, my research does not distinguish between *amici* that appear by leave of the parties from those who appear by leave of the Court. Nor does it distinguish between private *amici* and members of the Solicitor General's office. While there is evidence that the benefit of the SG and other government attorneys might simply arise from their prolific appearances before the Court (c.f. McGuire

[121] The original goal for chapter two was to collect data on four terms. The burden of collecting data about attorneys, however, meant that compromises had to be made.

1998), there is still the possibility that such attorneys might receive special treatment when it comes to appearing at argument as *amici*.

It also might be that the role oral *amici* play in supplementing inexperienced attorneys may be one aspect of a broader equalization function. Employing lower quality attorneys may or may not coincide with resource disadvantages on the part of the litigants themselves. There is reason to believe, though, that the role of *amici* might be attenuated by the identity of the litigants they support. Examining the success of litigants in state courts, Songer et al. found that resource-disadvantaged litigants—the so-called "have-nots" of Galanter's work—benefitted more from having *amici* supporting their side (Songer et al. 2000, 553; Galanter 1974). On the other hand, the "haves" experienced little change in their chances of prevailing. The implications for the research in this book are clear. A complete picture of the influence of oral *amici* should include information about the parties as well as about their attorneys. Properly capturing such data might reveal differential effects for when *amici* are likely to appear at argument, as well as for the actual impact they have on a case. The ability for friends at argument to impact whether the Court affirms or reverses might depend upon who they are supporting.

The research presented in chapter three, while supporting the idea that oral *amici* do influence the Court, also leaves plenty of unanswered questions and room for elaboration. Comparing my small set of cases to those that Johnson examined, it would appear that oral arguments become less important as one moves from cases without *amici*, to those with *amici*, and finally to cases with *amici* at argument. This effect might reflect one of three realities. First, as I suggest above, this might not reflect a demise in the value of argument but simply the reality of multiple citations when information sources proliferate. Second, it may be that I may be improperly measuring the value of argument. For the present discussion "less important" is defined in terms of the propensity for argument to be the sole source of the Court's holdings. Decreased solo citations only reflect one aspect of what argument contributes. Finally, we may have to admit that as an information gathering opportunity, oral arguments are in fact less important in some circumstances—chiefly those where the Court has less of an information need. The presence of oral *amici* might reflect one such condition. It could also be the case that when argument time is shared with additional attorneys, the Court has less opportunity to explore supplemental arguments. Further consideration is needed to properly determine which of these realities is correct.

There also remains room for refining the methods for detecting the impact that oral *amici* might have. The analysis in both chapters two and three would be improved by coding the types of questions addressed during argument (c.f. Johnson 2004, chapter 2). The impact of oral *amici* might be found in how the questions asked of *amicus* counsel differ from those asked of the parties—or how the presence of *amici* changes the questions that the justices ask of the parties. In both cases with and without friends, Johnson found that a large number of the questions at argument concern the preferences of external actors (Johnson 2004, 40–1). This may be less necessary when an external actor such as an interest group is actually present at argument. This approach could also be extended to the opinion analysis in chapter three. An interesting comparison might be had by looking at the overall types of points, such as threshold issues or policy concerns, and seeing if there were differing patterns in the sources those points are drawn from.

One final area for improvement lies in the particular methodology of chapter three. An analysis of the holdings in an opinion's syllabus may be the surest way to determine if the arguments advanced by *amici*—or by the litigants—are accepted by the Court. It might be too egalitarian, however, to presume that all syllabus points are created equal. Some points may be more controversial than others; some may simply lay the ground for a larger more important point. Ideally, each syllabus point could be categorized by its relative importance. Doing so might shed light on why some points in an opinion seem to have multiple sources while others do not, and why the Court chooses to spend its argument time on the issues that it does.[122]

Finally, the analysis of syllabus points could be expanded in two other directions inspired by Collins 2008. First, only looking at the Court's majority opinion might be short-changing the ability for oral

[122] In theory, it would be nice if oral arguments and the resulting court opinions could be compared using the same plagiarism detection software detailed in Corley 2008. On its face such an approach would encounter huge problems. Namely, it is difficult to imagine that opinion writers would copy whole sections of language verbatim from oral argument. This would require them to operate from argument transcripts as opposed to their own memory of the arguments. Further, textual analysis by itself is still flawed in that it does not take into account the tone or purpose of the "plagiarism" in question—something that is truly necessary for understanding *how* arguments get incorporated.

amici to have an impact. Minority opinions, while not policy in the formal sense, represent an important alternative to the actual Court opinion. In so much as a minority opinion often has the ability to become a majority opinion if sufficient votes change—or if over time the whole Court shifts toward a previous dissenting opinion—it seems relevant to consider whether oral *amici* have a special role to play in shaping the content of dissents. Second, the impact of oral *amici* might be seen in the consistency of the justices' votes. Collins' own research shows that the basic presence of *amici* in a case reduces the predictability of judicial behavior (Collins 2008, ch5). More *amici* mean more information. More information, in turn, means greater variance in how the Court responds to the information. If Collins' findings are true for *amici* participating by brief, it would seem likely that the presence of friends at argument could have a similar detectable effect on voting patterns.

WHAT IT ALL MEANS

Adding versus repeating information

In chapter one I discussed the ongoing debate in the *amicus* literature about whether third parties should focus on new information in their briefs or simply reiterate the arguments made by the parties. Despite the presumed authority of the law clerks Lynch interviewed on the matter (Lynch 2004), the results of my research in the previous chapter comport more with Spriggs and Wahlbeck 1997. Only a minority of the syllabus points appear to be drawn from *amicus* briefs but not those of the parties.[123]

This observation must be tempered with a reminder of the limitations of the research. As I explain in the discussion section of chapter three, an authoritative answer about whether *amici* should add or reiterate can only be answered by looking at all the points made in briefs and seeing which type of argument gets incorporated more. That more holdings appear to have multiple origins, and thus are "reiterated" claims, says little. In an *amicus* brief with ten repeated claims of which eight find their way into the opinion, it might be more impressive to discover

[123] Summing the relevant rows of Table 3.6 suggests that either alone or in conjunction with an information source other than party briefs, *amicus* briefs accounted for some fifteen percent of the holdings in the cases I examined. This number would be somewhat lower if one were to focus only on the *amici* that do not appear at argument.

that two of the brief's three innovative claims were accepted. Which is the greater win ratio? I also can neither confirm nor refute Collins' claim that novel information should be less accepted because it contributes to information overload (Collins 2008, 120).

More fundamentally, though, I believe that the *amicus* literature is misdirected in worrying about this debate. While the issue has a practical significance for Court practitioners wondering how to write their briefs, it goes no farther. The real fault lies in the presumption that reiterated information and novel information are on an equal footing. In reality, repeated information will always have the advantage. The Court simply cannot adopt every new piece of information brought to it. Cases like *Mapp* must be the exception and not the rule, or this debate would have long since been settled. In most instances the parameters of debate have been established by the parties' briefs and the factual record. *Amici* may offer alternative information but it is unlikely to alter the legal momentum of the case. Even in a single case, if two *amici* offer competing novel information, only one could in theory be successful.[124] Reiterating information is more likely to appear successful because the Court is already more likely to adopt the position in question.[125]

Rather than focusing on new information versus repeated information, I believe we need to consider what it is that leads to a given piece of information being used. To succeed in reshaping a case, any piece of information must be both relevant to the topic and must face a receptive Court. The best unit of analysis for these considerations might not be the individual holding or argument point, but rather the idea of an issue frame (Chong and Druckman 2007; Wedeking 2010). The parties, the various *amici*, and even the justices themselves attempt to provide the framework for viewing the case. It should be possible to see the ques-

---

[124] This discussion presumes that the defined definition of success would be to shape the outcome of the majority opinion. Once again, Collins offers an alternative perspective, noting that increased numbers of *amici* seem to lead to an increased number of separate opinions of any kind (Collins 2008, ch6). I would expect that the presence of *amici* at argument would compound this effect.

[125] If the question is no longer whether *amici* should add or repeat information, and if most *amici* are likely to have an effect on a case by offering a "me too" function, it would seem that added attention should be spent on the identity of the groups in question. Whether information from a brief gets used, even a brief that repeats information, may be influenced by the status or identity of the brief's filer.

tions justices ask, the points made in briefs, and the ultimate holdings in a case as specific expressions of competing frames. In any given case, the Court can consider only a few competing frames at most.

Uniting the Literature

This project sits at the intersection of at least three separate literatures: those of the *amicus curiae*, oral argument, and the impact of attorneys. I believe that my findings have clear implications for each. Insofar as the literature on *amici* has struggled to find consistent evidence that third parties can influence the judicial process, focusing on their presence at oral argument offers a new avenue for judging their value. While few *amici* will ever appear before the justices in person, when they do so they impact a case in noticeable ways. Future work will help explain the nature of that impact.

The implications are even greater for the literature on oral argument. The first generation of argument research was characterized by a focus on the behavior and performance of the justices. Researchers examined concepts such as "toughness" and "negative aspect" as a way to predict the outcome of a case (c.f. McFeeley and Ault 1979; Schubert et al. 1990, 1991a, 1991b, 1992). The biggest problem with this line of work was that studies tended to focus on a handful of cases, leading to questions about their external validity. To address this problem, the second generation of research on arguments shifted from small-N to larger–N studies that are more amenable to statistical modeling (c.f. Johnson 2001; Johnson 2004; Johnson et al. 2006). At the same time, these studies shifted from the justices' performance to measuring the content of what transpires at argument, such as the subject area of the justices' questions and the interrelationship between the justices (c.f. Johnson 2004; Johnson et al. 2008).

Even with the success of second generation research, the first generation's intuitive appeal is hard to ignore. On its face, it is easy to see why a justice asking harsh questions during argument might be important: in a potentially unfiltered way, it reflects the justices' attitudes about the parties. A number of recent studies have resurrected this logic. Greenhouse's fairly successful track record of predicting the outcomes of Supreme Court cases is certainly traceable to her observations during argument (Greenhouse 2004). A number of others have had similar predictive success (Roberts 2005; Shullman 2004; Wrightsman 2008)[126].

I would argue that we have now entered a third generation of argument research. Like first generation research, it focuses on how the behavior of the justices impacts the case. Like the second generation, though, it focuses on avoiding small case studies that have limited applicability. This young line of research has gone in at least two directions. The first is an attempt to verify earlier results. Johnson, Black, Goldman, and Treul have extended Roberts' question-counting analysis to examine some 2000 cases over an almost twenty year period (2009). Considering both the number of questions asked as well as the number of words used in argument, the authors found clear support for the conventional wisdom.

The more groundbreaking work in this area, conducted by the same authors, goes beyond the counting of questions. Still focusing on a large-N study, Johnson and his co-authors incorporate the insights from linguistic analysis to provide a theoretical grounding for the study of judicial emotion and affect (Johnson, Black, and Treul 2009; Johnson, Black, Goldman, and Treul 2009; Johnson, Black, Wedeking 2008; Johnson, Black, Wedeking 2009; also see Whissell 1989). As with the volume of questioning, their results are encouraging. While positive words do not seem to affect case outcomes, the use of negative language with a party contributes to that party's loss.

Other scholars have begun fine-tuning this research to categorize the purpose behind justices' questions—namely, to identify when justices appear to be pursuing information from the attorneys versus simply making a statement.[127] This research is especially important because it suggests questioning behavior may vary among the justices—complicating attempts to make simple and conclusive explanations of what transpires at oral argument. For example, from an individual standpoint not every justice votes against the party they question the most (Phillips and Carter 2009b). Confirming the importance of counsel, it appears that justices do seek more information from more experienced attorneys (Phillips and Carter 2009a). Regardless of the volume of questioning, only a sizable minority of justices vote against the side

---

[126] Wrightsman's research is somewhat different from the other two listed in that it also argues for including emotive content as part of the analysis.

[127] For a good synopsis of possible reasons that harsh questioning might point towards a party's defeat, see Epstein, Landes, and Posner 2009, 4.

they seek the most information from (Phillips and Carter 2009b). Interesting, the interaction between a justice's ideology and that of the party before them also appears to be important; some justices engage less with attorneys who are ideologically opposite (Phillips and Carter 2009a, 21).[128]

With a return to the study of judicial "performance," scholars have the opportunity to develop a holistic model of oral argument. The overall function of that hour where the attorneys face the justices is composed of both what justices do (second generation research) as well as how they do it (first and third generation). Both are needed because neither captures the entirety of the argument experience alone.

However, the model of oral argument is not complete without the results of this research. Examining the way in which justices might direct questions at each other, probe specific aspects of a case through their questions, or even tip their hand through their word choice ignores one basic fact. The justices are only half of oral argument. When a justice asks a question, whether rhetorical or not, some attorney stands at the lectern waiting to respond. Any analysis which focuses solely on the justices' performance neglects half the available data and makes the theoretical mistake of ignoring the interactive nature of argument. chapter two showed that understanding attorneys was key to understanding the presence of oral *amici*. The experience they do or do not bring to their cases affects whether they receive assistance at oral argument, and possibly whether they prevail in the case in the end.

Attorneys must be integrated into the new third generation research on oral arguments to address several outstanding questions or apparent paradoxes. For example, many studies have now confirmed that the party that gets asked more questions loses more often (Johnson, Black, Goldman, and Treul 2009; c.f. Epstein, Landes, and Posner 2009). At the same time, my research in chapter three shows that the side with oral *amici* tends to win. If the questions directed at *amici* are counted towards their party, should we see such cases as exceptions to the broader rule? Or is having a friend at argument an antidote to severe

---

[128] The Phillips and Carter research appears to be in its early phases and has yet to achieve the level of publication that other research has. Nonetheless, breaking down questioning behavior by justice remains an important addition to the literature. If the authors can find a way to systematize and organize the varying forces they argue are at play, it my prove nearly impossible for other scholars to argue that the proper level of analysis for oral argument is the case, as opposed to individual level.

questioning? Or, in such cases, does the side without the *amicus* still receive more intense questioning? Each of these possibilities is amenable to research and should be investigated.

Table 4.1: Possible Interactions Between the Behavior of Justices and Attorneys

1A Harsh Questioning Harsh Response	**1B** Gentle Questioning Harsh Response
2A Harsh Questioning Gentle Response	**2B** Gentle Questioning Gentle Response

Just as oral *amici* might temper the impact of harsh questioning, the attorneys themselves cannot be ignored. The new research on argument almost presumes the irrelevance of counsel. The length of questions and the harshness of words are weighed as if the same attorney argued each side in every case. Prior work has shown that the relative experience of attorneys can affect their chance of success in multiple ways. This is not currently reflected in the research on arguments, ignoring a number of interesting alternative situations. Justices may save especially lengthy questioning for attorneys with greater experience and, therefore, a greater ability to handle the longer questioning. Harsh questioning might fall more on attorneys with limited experience pushing claims beyond their reasonable limit. In many ways the actual experience and quality of the advocacy provided might temper the impact that the justices' questioning will have on the case's disposition.

In a similar vein, it seems essential to extend emotional affect and question count analysis directly to parties' counsel. Doing so would show if an attorney's success depends on how long they spoke or how emotionally charged their responses were—even accounting for their level of experience. At the moment it appears that an attorney caught in the justices' crosshairs is most likely going to lose; this situation is represented by the shaded boxes of Table 4.1. With further research that conclusion might still be valid. However, it is possible that failure is the product of both the justices' questions and the attorneys' responses. The only box in Table 4.1 with an increased likelihood of failure might actually be 1A—or more interestingly, 1B.

By and large, the most important reason for including attorneys in oral research is to plumb the interactive nature of what occurs during argument. Rather than presuming that justices will independently either be harsh or gentle in their methods and attorneys likewise, it makes more sense to presume that the behavior of the two groups is codependent. An argument need not begin hostile. The Court may very well be moved in a skeptical or antagonistic direction because of the manner in which an attorney presents her case. That hostility might escalate if the response from counsel is similarly hostile. Conversely, a tense situation might be defused by a properly chosen response—something that a practiced attorney might be far more able to provide. In each instance, sampling only the justices' behavior and presuming it to be constant over the course of the argument ignores the dynamics that may be at work.

If oral arguments should be studied as an interactive phenomenon, it would seem important to rethink the unit of analysis for such research. Basing studies on discrete questions from the justices does have a certain logic. Questions are fairly easily identifiable and can be categorized relatively easily.[129] Counting the number of words used is also intuitive, since it provides a measure of the length of discourse inde-

---

[129] While I have in mind here the types of categories that Johnson uses to determine the subject of the question, others have attempted to categorize questions in other ways. Phillips and Carter conducted an initial study which included placing the justices' questions on a six-point scale that ranged from substantial questions designed to elicit substantial responses (so-called "wh-questions") to rhetorical declarations (Phillips and Carter 2009d).

pendent of the speaker's speed. But both techniques do have their drawbacks. The number of words spoken serves to measure a number of other unrelated phenomena, including their verbosity, behavioral differences among the Court's changing membership, and evolving norms about the use of argument time (c.f. Johnson, Black, and Treul 2009, 9 figure 2). Focusing only on explicit questions also misses the possibility that the discourse during argument may be furthered through declarative statements or by questions that are linked to each other in less than obvious ways.

These comments might seem critical of what I have called the third generation of oral argument research. Given that this era of large-N, empirically grounded analysis of argument performance is still quite young, my only goal is to point out what I believe must happen to maximize its impact. Questions and word counts might have their place, but a full understanding of oral argument needs a hybrid approach that emphasizes the connections between questions and answers, as well as the individuals on both sides of the bench.

Some of the claims made here about oral argument research also show the potential for expanding the literature on attorneys. Chapter two discussed several of the measures scholars have developed for attorney quality. What is notable is that most of these are proxy measures, attempting to get at quality indirectly through something like an attorney's attendance at an elite law school. Finding a direct indicator of quality proves to be much more difficult. Once the work on oral argument has been expanded to include data on what attorneys actually do in a case, it may be possible to develop new measures of attorney quality based on the actions they take and the choices they make in arguing a case.[130]

ORAL *AMICI* AND THE SWING VOTER

In chapter one I discussed Justice Owen Roberts' vote in *West Coast Hotel Co. v. Parrish*, where Roberts served as a "swing voter," a justice who finds himself caught between two competing blocks of colleagues and thus is able to serve as the deciding vote in a case. While not every

[130] It seems reasonable to presume that the idea of attorney quality will always be controversial enough that a single measure of quality may never be found. By gauging the justices' responses and the ultimate outcomes in cases, it does seem likely that a list of "best practices" could be compiled that would at least give guidance as to how attorneys could put the best foot forward.

swing by a swing voter ends up reshaping the whole direction of the Court like Justice Roberts did, their presence is often most noticeable in landmark cases. Schmidt and Yalof identify a number of such cases for Justice Kennedy, widely seen as the current swing on the Court (2004, 210; c.f. Toobin 2005, Barnes 2007). Though appointed by the quintessential conservative of the late twentieth century, many of Kennedy's most visible decisions have paired him with the Court's more liberal wing. *Planned Parenthood v. Casey*, for example, was supposed to be the case that turned back the tide of abortion for social conservatives. In the end, the plurality opinion upheld basic holdings of *Roe*, disappointing many who had conservative expectations for Kennedy.

Many have been prompted to take a closer look at Kennedy's jurisprudence to determine why he has been such a surprise. Summarizing these comments, Greenhouse notes that descriptions of Kennedy have ranged from "agenda-free moderate" to "thoughtful libertarian" (Greenhouse 1996; Schmidt and Yalof 2004). These varying labels hint at the diversity of reasons that could explain the behavior of a swing voter. To call Kennedy a libertarian, on the one hand, ascribes to him a fairly strong ideological stance that simply happens to differ from others on the Court and which, hence, may have unpredictable interactions with the other justices' ideologies. On the other hand, to suggest Kennedy is an agenda-free moderate is to say that pure ideological motivations might have less of an influence on his decision making.[131] What is true of Kennedy is likely true of other swing justices as well, and perhaps even true of more "stable" justices. Ideology has proven a fairly reliable indicator of the justices' votes (c.f. Segal and Spaeth 1993; Segal and Spaeth 2002). It is always a possibility, though, that the construct by which we measure ideology may fail to accurately describe a

[131] Referring to someone as a "moderate" does not in and of itself suggest the individual lacks ideology. True, being moderate is often taken as a sign of decreased commitment to either the liberal or conservative points of view. In recent years—perhaps in line with patterns of partisan dealignment—there has been an increased tendency to treat "moderates" as espousing some fairly specified set of beliefs that happens to exist between the traditional poles. Each of these meanings for the term "moderate" would suggest a different interpretation of Kennedy's motivations. Without intending to further on the discussion in any meaningful way, I choose to adopt the first meaning for moderate, based in part on the use of the term "agenda-free."

justice with truly divergent beliefs.[132] A simple measure of ideology may also mask instances in which a justice may be open to extra-ideological considerations.

Understanding swing voters

The eyes of judicial scholars may have been focused on swings for some time. However, there are still a number of difficulties with making sense of the swing phenomenon. Schmidt and Yalof identify a number such problems in their article "The 'Swing Voter Revisited'" (2004). The first is simply identifying what might be an example of swing behavior. Swing voters are, in essence, pivotal voters. The ability to pivot depends upon the Court as a whole, for example, on the size and number of voting blocs. In this regard, Justice Roberts' famous switch in the 1930s stands as a true outlier in the Court's history. The well-known division between the traditional and New Deal factions on the Court represented a clear ideological split even more pronounced than the current division between liberals and conservatives. Not every opportunity for a change of heart is so obvious or so public. Sometimes a purposeful switch by a member of the Court might only be recognized after the fact, by relying upon their notes and records. And the most common way of determining who is most likely to swing—identifying when justices are disproportionately in the majority—may itself be flawed. A frequent member of the majority might either be an independently-minded swing voter, or might simply be adept at persuading others to form coalitions (Schmidt and Yalof 2004, 211–2).

The attempt to find the "right" way to identify swings has actually become something of a cottage industry in judicial politics. An anonymous article in the 1949 Stanford Law Review took the first crack at a standard, arguing that a swing could arise when there were two equal

---

[132] Measures of the ideology of Supreme Court members base their rankings on a scale that ranges from very conservative to very liberal. Some scholars of ideology propose that the concept may be more complex than just that basic unidimensional dynamic (c.f. Hinich and Munger 1994; Gerring 1997). A justice whose ideology is best measured by some scale tangential or parallel to the conservative/liberal dimension may be tagged as a moderate precisely because that scale fails to render a consistent categorization of their thought, capturing a rough balance of instances where the justice appears to vote conservatively and liberally. To expand upon the taxonomy above, this suggests another interpretation of "moderate" in which the real ideology is translated into the "shadow" ideology of moderateness.

and counterbalancing blocs on the Court, plus a middle justice who is "reasonably susceptible of being attracted to either" (Anonymous 1949, 718).[133] The first abstraction from this archetype was Schultz and Howard's focus on the movement of justices between blocs, regardless of the size of said blocs (1975). While swings are usually sought in 5 to 4 cases, swings could arise in cases decided 6 to 3 or even 7 to 2; such cases may actually be distinguished by the presence of multiple swing voters (Blasecki 1990, 533). Under this conception, the important part is not necessarily the swing's ability to determine the outcome of the case, but simply the fact that there are justices with loose affiliations who may move between the sides in a case. Not many scholars have gone so far as to adopt Schultz and Howard's abstraction, because as one author has put it "While this approach may identify 'swing justices,' it …empties the swing voting concept of much of its explanatory value" (Blasecki 1990, 533).

Others have sought to refine their understanding of swing voters by being as precise as possible about what qualifies a justice to be a swing. Edelman and Chen prefer to think of things in terms of the most "powerful" justice, a title they award based on a calculated "power index" of when justices were or could theoretically have been in the majority (1996). This system has met with substantial criticism from Lynn Baker, who takes particular issue with the complex way the authors examine potential coalitions (Baker 1996, 192–4). Baker offers a number of alternative measures, each simpler than Edelman and Chen's. The controversy between the two sets of authors epitomizes the challenges to be had in defining a swing vote. In their response to Baker, Edelman and Chen survey the literature and suggest that scholars are operating with at least three separate concepts. Fairly well defined is the idea of the median voter, one who is placed ideologically at the center of his or her colleagues. In their articles, Edelman and Chen have sought to develop a different concept, the most powerful or most "dangerous" justice, the one with the greatest ability to steer the outcome of the Court's choices. In their words, the disagreements in the literature all center around the idea of the swing voter, and how a given academic defines the swing—as either the median or the most powerful justice (Edelman and Chen 1996b).

---

[133] The astute will notice that in some ways this definition jumps the gun, positing that it is a middle justice who is able to become the swing voter.

Another complication with understanding swing voters is the question of how large the scope of inquiry should be. Schmidt and Yalof argue that most previous studies of swing voting tried to encompass too many different types of cases. While scholars do so in order to come up with the most synoptic commentary on the role of a particular justice with the Court, lumping all cases together has the effect of erasing the evidence of nuance in individual jurisprudence. In their own study, the authors focus on the area of civil liberties, driven in part by the conventional wisdom that Justice Kennedy has both a reputation for his swing tendencies in the area as well as a number of high-profile free speech opinions under his belt.[134] What the two find is a bit surprising. Over the time period they studied, Justice O'Connor actually had a better overall claim to being the swing justice on questions of civil liberties (Schmidt and Yalof 2004, 214). Within the even more focused area of free speech cases, though, Kennedy appears as the swing par *excellence.* In such cases he is the most liberal member of the five justice conservative bloc, but also is more likely to join the three most liberal members of the Court than even Justice Breyer is. Over the almost two-dozen free speech cases decided during his tenure on the Court, Kennedy has been in the majority 86.4% of the time—a record for the period (Schmidt and Yalof 2004, 215). The authors extrapolate from this finding to suggest that a more focused analysis of swings in particular areas of law might show that there more swing voters than research traditionally shows. In addition, the list of justices who serve as swings may be longer than expected, with Breyer, Rehnquist, and even Scalia serving as swing voters under the right circumstances (Schmidt and Yalof 2004, 216).

That, of course, simply begs the question of which circumstances can trigger swing behavior. Mishler and Sheehan, based on an analysis of cases over a forty year period, argue that differing levels of ideological commitment will condition a justice's response to non-ideological stimuli. Moderate justices, it would appear, are most likely to be receptive to the influence of public opinion (Mishler and Sheehan 1996, 197). Because moderate justices are often in a position to cast a swing vote, public opinion has the potential to play a large role in shaping the Court's opinions. The authors do caution, though, that what may appear

---

[134] The authors list his concurrence in *Texas v. Johnson,* and his opinions in *Ward v. Rock Against Racism* (1989), *ISKCON v. Lee* (1992), *Edenfield v.* Fane (1993), *Florida Bar v. Went for It, Inc.* (1995), and Ashcroft *v. ACLU* (2002).

to be swings or voting changes on the part of the Court may also be the result of the Court's changing agenda—and not necessarily a change on the part of the justices (Mishler and Sheehan 1996, 197).

What difference does it make?

Swing voters are an accepted fact of judicial reality. But is the struggle to define the concept anything more than academic theatrics? Is there any harm in operating with a lazy definition of the swing voter? At least two responses suggest themselves.

First, understanding what makes a swing voter influential is important for a full understanding of the Court as an institution. Schmidt and Yalof suggest three different types of individuals who may wield power on the Court (2004, 209). The first is the Chief Justice, who by virtue of opinion assignment and other institutional norms can exert pressure on case outcomes. The second category is the justice who either through force of personality or intellect can forge coalitions with colleagues. The third is the swing voter. While any member of a nine-person Court has some degree of influence, these three categories describe the special influence that members of the Court may come to hold in the right circumstances. Without a proper understanding of the swing voter, any picture of the Court is incomplete. Perhaps a bit facetiously, Baker suggests that the best advice to a new justice hoping to be influential is to become the "joiner"—to be in the majority as often as possible (1996, 208).

Perhaps the more important reason for pursuing a precise definition of swing voting is that common sense often fails. Basing her work off an early version of the Segal/Spaeth database, Blasecki sought to examine the conventional wisdom that Justice Powell had been a moderate swing justice during his time on the Court (1990, 531). Rather than confirm this, Blasecki's research suggests that Powell was actually a staunch conservative throughout his entire tenure (1990, 538). The perception of his moderate tendencies and ability to serve as a swing vote hinge entirely on a small number of nonrepresentative civil liberties cases decided in a liberal direction across the 1970s and 1980s, in which Powell was often in the five-person majority (Blasecki 1990, 531, 545).

The impact of swings, writ large

Swing voters are of obvious importance because of their potential to alter the outcome of a case. When taken in the aggregate, they become even more significant. A change of heart could signal an entire change in the course of the Court's jurisprudence. These are the same concerns that arise whenever a vacancy occurs on the Court. It is well accepted that presidents will fill openings with jurists who are ideologically compatible with themselves. And most presidents get a chance to do so; Chen calculates the odds of a one-term president being able to make at least one appointment at 86.3% (2003, 704).[135]

Even apart from considerations of whether justices will change their ideology over time, nominating a new justice is a far cry from actually reshaping policy. Not long after Justice Souter announced his retirement in the spring of 2009, journalists were already reporting that Obama's nominee would be unlikely to alter the Court's decisions (c.f. Richey 2009). Similar stories appeared after Justice Stevens' announced retirement (Stolberg and Savage 2010; Liptak 2010). President Obama's two appointments took place in very different circumstances. Justice Sotomayor won confirmation from a Senate safe in Democratic hands; Justice Kagan's appointment faced the possibility of a Republican filibuster after the special election that placed Republican Scott Brown into the seat formerly held by Ted Kennedy. Despite that difference, neither appointment reshaped the face of the Court. In both cases, a solid member of the liberal bloc was replaced with another liberal justice, resulting in little impact on the Court's five to four decisions. The situation would be different if Kennedy were to step down—much as scholars wondered how an O'Connor departure would have played out if the results of the 2004 presidential election had differed (Martin, Quinn, and Epstein 2005).[136]

---

[135] A recent wave of excellent research has begun to focus on Supreme Court confirmation hearings themselves. See Bybee 2011; Cottrill et al 2010; Peretti 2008; Farganis and Wedeking. Conventional wisdom about confirmation hearings holds two things: 1) recent nominations have become more contentious than those in the past; and 2) recent nominees have become more evasive in the face of questioning by senators. Perhaps the most valuable insight of this new round of research is that the conventional wisdom appears to be incorrect on both counts.

[136] Perhaps going beyond what Martin, Quinn, and Epstein had envisioned, George W. Bush was able to replace both justices they discussed in their article. Rehnquist's replacement with Roberts did prove to change little about the

This logic represents the traditional view of Supreme Court appointments, under which every nomination is of immense symbolic importance but only a few end up having an immediate impact on the Court.[137] The most interesting recent work on median justices challenges some of these assumptions. Epstein and Jacobi have sought to draw a distinction between justices who simply find themselves at the middle of the Court, and those who are actually able to capitalize on their position of potential power. The authors refer to the latter category as "super medians" (Epstein and Jacobi 2008, 41).

Two factors appear to control whether a median justice is able to rise to super status. One is the size of the "gap" that separates the median justice from those on either side. Relatedly, the power of the median is moderated by the extent to which her preferences do or do not "overlap" with those of the surrounding justices. Together, these factors distinguish between a median who happens to be the center justice out of a block of moderates or a "leaning" member of one ideological wing of the Court, versus a median who truly stands apart and separate from both sides of the Court (Epstein and Jacobi 2008, 43). It is this latter type of justice that has the potential to become a super median. According to the standards for gap and overlap, the authors find that Kennedy and O'Connor both qualify as super-medians.

Epstein and Jacobi's research suggests two changes to conventional wisdom. The first is that the overall tenor of the Court *could* be changed without replacing the median. In their article, the authors look explicitly at what for them was a hypothetical scenario in which President Obama was able to replace David Souter (Epstein and Jacobi 2008, 94). Though he himself was not the median, he was ideologically proximate, compared to the justices at the extremes of the ideological spectrum. Therefore, whoever his replacement was would have an impact on the gap and ideological overlap at the center of the Court. One strategy for Obama would have been to choose a fairly moderate nomi-

---

Court's decisions. Alito's replacement of O'Connor has been more interesting. While he certainly occupies a more conservative position on the Court, the real legacy of his appointment has not been an unabashed swing to the right for the Court, but rather the enthroning of Anthony Kennedy as the median swing voter.

[137] Ruckman 1993 stands as a good discussion of this traditional view. For more recent work on the role of strategy in choosing Supreme Court nominees, see also Krehbiel 2007; Cameron, Park, and Beim 2008; Kastellec et al 2010; Peretti 2008; Rohde and Shepsle 2007; Scott and Martinek 2009.

nee who would impinge on Kennedy's ideological ground. Doing so would serve to dilute Kennedy's power, perhaps downgrading him from super median status to that of a regular medina. Conversely, if Obama were to have chosen a more markedly liberal nominee, Kennedy's power in future terms might actually be increased because the distance between the two blocs on the Court would be that much larger (Epstein and Jacobi 2008, 94).

Figure 4.1: The Effect of Obama's Appointments to the Supreme Court, Measured by Segal/Cover Scores

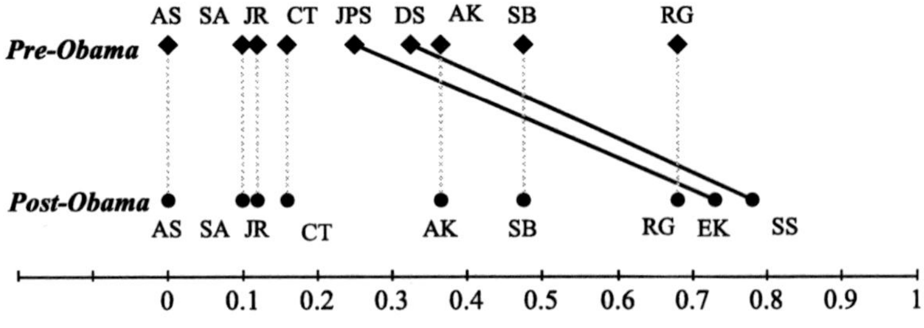

Information on Obama's two appointees is still forthcoming and it is not yet possible to fully assess how they will change the Court's ideological landscape. As of the time this book went to press, the more valuable Martin/Quinn scores of judicial ideology had only been updated to reflect Justice Sotomayor's first term. Her score of –0.229 marks her as more moderate than Justice Souter in his last term (–1.124), but her score will likely trend in a more liberal direction once additional terms are included.[138] The static and therefore less useful Segal/Cover scores have been updated.[139] Justice Sotomayor rates a

[138] The most current Martin/Quinn scores can be found on their website, http://mqscores.wustl.edu/

[139] See the discussion of data in chapter three for more information on the differences between the two scales for judicial ideology. In short, Martin/Quinn scores are preferred because they are dynamically adjusted to account for possible changes in judicial behavior over a tenure on the Court. Segal/Cover scores are static and based on the perceived ideology of the nominee before their appointment. Stevens and Souter are two clear examples of how a nomi-

0.78 compared to Souter's 0.325 (higher numbers reflect an evaluation of the potential justice as more liberal); Kagan's score of 0.730 marks her as far more liberal than Stevens, at 0.250. Given the problems inherent in such scores, any differences in ideologies of the Court's two most recent hires compared to their predecessors should be taken with several grains of salt. It is very possible, though, that Obama's appointments—even if they prove to be very liberal—may have the effect of reinforcing the power wielded by Justice Kennedy. Figures 4.1 and 4.2 project the makeup of the Court before and after Obama's appointments. To maximize his influence on the Court by reducing the influence of Anthony Kennedy, Justices Sotomayor and Kagan would need to have ideologies somewhere in the range between Breyer and Kennedy, represented by horizontal dark black line in Figure 4.2.

Figure 4.2: The Effect of Obama's Appointments to the Supreme Court, Measured by Martin/Quinn Scores

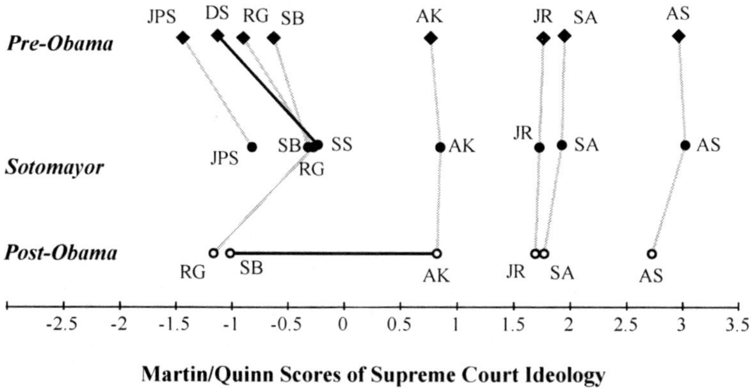

* Pre-Obama values are based on the data for the 2008 term prior to Sotomayor's arrival. The second row shows values with the new justice's initial Martin/Quinn score, which will likely change as terms unfold. Post-Obama values are based on five-year averages of M/Q scores for the returning justices.

---

nee perceived to be fairly moderate can end up behaving in more extreme a manner than expected.

The second implication of super median research is that attorneys need not always feel compelled to pitch cases to the median justice (c.f. McAtee and McGuire 2007, 275). In situations where a number of justices are clustered at the center of the spectrum, or where the preferences of relatively moderate justices overlap, the Court's median will be comparatively weak. This opens the possibility of what Epstein and Jacobi call "alternative majorities"—winning coalitions of justices that exclude the median (2008, 97).

Alternative majorities are likely to form when some consideration other than ideological policy preferences is able to bring justices into agreement. Recognized examples of such factors include federalism and a justice's preferred mode of interpretation (Epstein and Jacobi 2008, 96–7; Baird and Jacobi 2005). Given the findings in this book, I would suggest adding the presence of oral *amici* to the list. When friends of the Court are allowed to appear with the parties at argument, justices across the spectrum alter their voting habits, voting with less ideological consistency. Most relevant for the discussion here, though, is the even more pronounced influence that oral *amici* have on moderate justices.

While the full reason for this effect has not yet been determined, its implications for Court practitioners are as clear and significant as those of Epstein and Jacobi. Successfully winning a case may mean appealing to the swing justice who will secure a Court majority. The nature of this appeal need not be a simple "love letter" framing the case in the precise ideological tone designed to capture the swing (c.f. Barnes 2007). Attorneys may be better served by marshaling the support of third parties to provide a broader or richer presentation of their case. This approach may serve to attract not only the swing justice but enough other moderate justices to secure an alternative majority.

This book has shown that oral *amici* are an important frontier in the quest to demonstrate the impact had by friends of the court. Their presence is not entirely random, and in fact seems to equalize representation, either when the parties are differently resourced or represented by inexperienced attorneys. More significantly, their involvement can have an effect on both the case's disposition and the holdings established in the majority opinion. But even when unsuccessful—as with Texas' appearance at argument in the death penalty case of *Kennedy v. Louisiana*—their presence suggests that more than simple ideology may be at work in the Court's decision making.

APPENDIX 1

Amici that participated in more than one oral argument (1953–1985)

Group	# of Cases
United States	276
Securities and Exchange Commission	19
State of California	13
AFL-CIO	8
City of New York	7
National Labor Relations Board	5
American Civil Liberties Union	3
State of Oregon	3
State of Florida	3
Commodity Futures Trading Commission	3
State of Wyoming	3
State of Texas	3
State of Iowa	3
Federal Communications Commission	2
State of New Hampshire	2
American Arbitration Association	2
State of New Jersey	2
State of Washington	2
State of Alabama	2
National Association of Supervisors of State Banks	2
National Association of Food Chains	2
Chamber of Commerce of the United States of America	2
American Optometric Association	2
State of North Carolina	2

APPENDIX 2

Amici that participated in only one oral argument (1953–1985)

American Blood Resources Association
American Council of Life Insurance
American Psychiatric Association
Americans for Public Schools
City of Mobile, Alabama
Cleveland Burgess
Coalition of National Voluntary Organizations
Compania Azucarera Vertientes-Camaguey de Cuba
Confederated Tribes of the Colville Indian Reservation
Congress of Industrial Organizations
Dewey County, South Dakota
Equal Employment Opportunity Commission
Fed. Comm. Defender Organization of the Legal Aid
Federal Home Loan Bank Board
Federal Power Commission
Governors Conference
Guild of Prescription Opticians of America, inc.
Independent Natural Gas Association of America
Interstate Commerce Commission
Japanese American Citizens League
Judges of the Court of Claims
Lawyers Committee for Civil Rights Under Law
Memphis City Schools
Michigan Bell Telephone Company
Multi State Tax Commission
NAACP Legal Defense and Educational Fund, inc.
National Agricultural Chemicals Association

National Assn. of Retail Grocers of the United States
National Association of Broadcasters
National Association of Realtors
National Broadcasting Company, inc.
National Council of Juvenile Court Judges
National Jewish Commission on Law and Public Affairs
National Org. of Women Legal Defense and Education
National Rural Electric Cooperative Association
New York Clearing House Association
New York County District Attorney
New York State Athletic Commission
NY Times Display Advertising Salesmen Steering Cmt.
Ohio Association of Juvenile Court Judges
Pennsylvania Savings and Loan League
Planned Parenthood Federation of America, inc.
Puerto Rico
Radio Station WAIT, Chicago
Register of Copyrights
Republic of France
Secretary of Labor
State Mutual Life Insurance Comp. of Massachusetts
State of Arkansas
State of Colorado
State of Idaho
State of Illinois
State of Maryland
State of Nebraska
State of Oklahoma
State of Vermont
Supreme Court of Pennsylvania
Twin Lakes Reservoir and Canal Company
United States Court of Claims
United States Court of Customs and Patent Appeals
United States Senate
University of New York

References

Atkins v. *Virginia*. 2002. 536 U.S. 304.

Coker v. *Georgia*. 1977. 433 U.S. 584.

Grutter v. *Bollinger*. 2003. 539 U.S. 306.

Kennedy v. *Louisiana*. 2008. 554 U.S. 407.

McLain v. Real Estate Board of New Orleans. 1980. 444 U.S. 232.

Mobil Oil Corp v. Commissioner of Taxes. 1980. 445 U.S. 425.

National Foundation v. City of Fort Worth. 1969. 415 F.2d 41.

Neonatology Associates, P.A. v. C.I.R. 2002. 293 F.3d 128.

Puyallup Tribe v. Department of Game of Washington et al. 1968. 391 U.S. 392.

Roper v. *Simmons*. 2005. 543 U.S. 551.

Uttecht v. Brown. 2007. 551 U.S. 1.

Village of Schaumburg v. Citizens for a Better Environment. 1980. 444 U.S. 620.

Adler, Matthew D. 1997. "Judicial Restraint in the Administrative State: Beyond the Countermajoritarian Difficulty." *University of Pennsylvania Law Review* 145 (4): 759–892.

Angell, Ernest. 1967. "The Amicus Curiae American Development of English Institutions." *The International and Comparative Law Quarterly* 16 (October): 1017–1044.

Aumann, Robert J. and Sergiu Hart. 2003. "Long Cheap Talk." *Econometrica* 71 (November): 1619–1660.

Austen, David, Smith, and William H. Riker. 1987. "Asymmetric Information and the Coherence of Legislation." *American Political Science Review* 81 (September): 897-918.

Axelrod, Robert. 1970. Conflict of Interest: A Theory of Divergent Goals with Applications to Politics. Chicago: Markham.

Bailey, Michael A. and Forrest Maltzman. 2005. "Inter-branch Communication: When Does the Court Solicit Executive Branch Views?" Presented at the Annual Meeting of the Midwest Political Science Association, Chicago.

Bailey, Michael and Kelly H. Chang. 2001. "Comparing Presidents, Senators, and Justices: Interinstitutional Preference Estimation." *Journal of Law, Economics & Organization* 17 (2): 477-508.

Bailey, Michael, Brian Kamoie, and Forrest Maltzman. 2004. "Signals from the Tenth Justice: The Political Role of the Solicitor General in Supreme Court Decision-making."

Bailey, Michael. 2003. "Bridging Institutions: Bayesian Common Space Preference Estimates for Presidents, Senators, and Justices, 1946-2002." Georgetown University. Manuscript.

Baker, Stewart A. 1984. "A Practical Guide to Certiorari." The Catholic University Law Review 33 (Spring): 611.

Banks, Jeffrey and Joel Sobel. 1987. "Equilibrium Selection in Signaling Games." Econometrica 55 647–662.

Barker, Lucius J. 1967. "Third Parties in Litigation: A Systematic View of the Judicial Function." Journal of Politics 29 (1): 41-69.

Barnes, Robert. 2007. "Justice Kennedy: The Highly Influential Man in the Middle." *Washington Post*, May 13.

Barnum, David G. 1985. "The Supreme Court and Public Opinion: Judicial Decision Making in the Post-New Deal Period." The Journal of Politics 47 (June): 652–666.

Barrett, Gerald V. and Scott B. Morris. 1993. "The American Psychological Association's Amicus Curiae Brief in Price Waterhouse v. Hopkins: The Values of Science versus the Values of the Law." Law and Human Behavior 17 (April): 201-215.

Baum, Lawrence. 1994. "Symposium: The Supreme Court and the Attitudinal Model." Law and Courts 4 (Spring): 3-5.

Baum, Lawrence. 2001. The Supreme Court. Seventh Edition. Washington, D.C.: CQ Press.

Baumgartner, Frank R. and Beth L. Leech. 1998. *Basic Interests: The Importance of Groups in Politics and Political Science*. Princeton, NJ: Princeton University Press.

Behuniak–Long, Susan. 1991. "Friendly Fire: Amici Curiae and Webster v. Reproductive Health Services." *Judicature* 74 261–270.

Benesh, Sara C. and Malia Reddick. 2002. "Overruled—An Event History Analysis of Lower Court Reaction to Supreme Court Alteration of Precedent"." *The Journal of Politics* 64 (May): 534-550.

Bennett, Robert W. 2001. "Counter-Conversationalism and the Sense of Difficulty." *Northwestern University Law Review* 95 (3): 845–906.

Benoit, William. 1989. "Attorney Argumentation and Supreme Court Opinions." *Argumentation and Advocacy* 26 22-38.

Berman, Daniel M. 1966. *It Is So Ordered: The Supreme Court Rules on School Segregation*. New York: W. W. Norton and Company, Inc.

Berry, Mary Frances. 1978. *Stability, Security, and Continuity: Mr. Justice Burton and Decision-Making in the Supreme Court, 1945-1958*. Westport, CT: Greenwood Press.

Bickel, Alexander M. 1962. *The Least Dangerous Branch: The Supreme Court at the Bar of Politics*. Second Edition, 1986. New Haven, CT: Yale University Press.

Biskupic, Joan. 1999. "Sparring with the Supreme Court Nine." *Washington Post* November 1: A25.

Biskupic, Joan. 2006. "Justices Make Points by Questioning Lawyers." *U.S.A. Today* October 6: 7A.

Black, Ryan C., Timothy R. Johnson, Justin Wedeking. 2010. "Can Justices Predict Case Outcomes at Oral Arguments?" Presented at the Annual Meeting of the American Political Science Association, Washington D.C.

Bohman, James and William Rehg, ed. 1997. *Deliberative Democracy: Essays on Reason and Politics*. Cambridge, MA: The MIT Press.

Bork, Robert H. 1991. *The Tempting of America: The Political Seduction of the Law*. New York: Free Press.

Boucher, Robert L., Jr. and Jeffrey A. Segal. 1995. "Supreme Court Justices as Strategic Decision Makers—Aggressive Grants and Defensive Denials on the Vinson Court." *The Journal of Politics* 57 (August): 824–837.

Bowen, Lauren. 1995. "Do Court Decisions Matter?" In *Contemplating Courts*, Washington, DC: Congressional Quarterly Books, 376-389.

Brenner, Saul and Marc Stier. 1996. "Retesting Segal and Spaeth's Stare Decisis Model." *American Journal of Political Science* 40 (Nov.): 1036-1048.

Brenner, Saul, Timothy M. Hagle, and Harold J. Spaeth. 1989. "The Defection of the Marginal Justice on the Warren Court." *The Western Political Quarterly* 42 (Sep.): 409-425.

Breyer, Stephen. 1998. "The Interdependence of Science and Law." *Judicature* 82 (1): 24-27.

Brinkmann, Beth S. 2003. "A First Argument in the Tradition of Many." *The Journal of Appellate Practice and Process* (March): 61–73.

Brisbin, Richard A., Jr. 1996. "Slaying the Dragon: Segal, Spaeth and the Function of Law in Supreme Court Decision Making." *American Journal of Political Science* 40 (Nov.): 1004-1017.

Budziak, Jeffrey and Daniel Lempert. 2010. "Legal Argumentation and Case Quality at the U.S. Supreme Court " 5th Annual Conference on Empirical Legal Studies Paper. Available at SSRN: http://ssrn.com/abstract=1636562.

Bybee, Keith J. 2011. "Will the Real Elena Kagan Please Stand Up? Conflicting Public Images in the Supreme Court Confirmation Process." *Wake Forest Journal of Law & Policy* 1 (1): 137-155.

Caldeira, Gregory A. 1991. "Courts and Public Opinion." In *The American Courts: A Critical Assessment*, ed. John B. Gates and Charles A. Johnson. Washington, D.C.: CQ Press, np.

Caldeira, Gregory A. and James L. Gibson. 1992. "The Etiology of Public Support for the Supreme Court." *American Journal of Political Science* 36 (August): 635-664.

Caldeira, Gregory A. and John R. Wright. 1988. "Organized Interests and Agenda Setting in the U.S. Supreme Court." *American Political Science Review* 82 (4): 1109-1127.

Caldeira, Gregory A. and John R. Wright. 1990. "Amici Curiae before the Supreme Court: Who Participates, When, and How Much?" *Journal of Politics* 52 (3): 782-806.

Caldeira, Gregory and Christopher J. W. Zorn. 1998. "Of Time and Consensual Norms in the Supreme Court." *American Journal of Political Science* 42 (July): 874–902.

Calvert, Randall. 1985. "The Value of Biased Information: A Rational Choice Model of Political Advice." *Journal of Politics* 47 (June): 530-55.

Cameron, Charles M. 1994. "Decision-Making and Positive Political Theory (Or, Using Game Theory to Study Judicial Politics)." Presented at the meeting of the Columbus Conference, Columbus, OH.

Cameron, Charles M., Albert D. Cover, and Jeffrey A. Segal. 1990. "Senate Voting on Supreme Court Nominees: A Neoinstitutional Model." *The American Political Science Review* 84 (Jun.): 525-534.

Cameron, Charles, Jee-Kwan Park, and Deborah Beim. 2008. "Shaping Supreme Court Policy Through Appointments: The Impact of a New Justice." *Minnesota Law Review* 93: 1820.

Cameron, Charles M., Jeffrey A. Segal, and Donald Songer. 2000. "Strategic Auditing in a Political Hierarchy: An Informational Model of the Supreme Court's Certiorari Decisions." *The American Political Science Review* 94 (Mar.): 101-116.

Cammisa, Anne Marie. 1995. *Governments as Interest Groups: Intergovernmental Lobbying and the Federal System*. N.p.: Praeger Publishers.

Canon, Bradley C. and Charles A. Johnson. 1999. *Judicial Policies: Implementation and Impact.* Washington, D.C.: CQ Press.

Caplan, Lincoln. 1987. *The Tenth Justice: The Solicitor General and the Rule of Law*. New York: Vintage Books.

Casper, Jonathan D. 1976. "The Supreme Court and National Policy Making." *The American Political Science Review* 70 (March): 50-63.

Chen, Paul H.S. 2006. "Amici Curiae Influence on Supreme Court Decision-making in Gonzales v. Raich." SSRN, http://ssrn.com/abstract=913443. Manuscript.

Chong, Dennis and James N. Druckman. 2007. "Framing Theory." *Annual Review of Political Science* 10 (June): 103–126.

Choper, Jesse L. 1980. *Judicial Review and the National Political Process: A Functional Reconsideration of the Role of the Supreme Court*. Chicago: University of Chicago Press.

Clark, Peter B. and James Q. Wilson. 1961. "Incentive Systems: A Theory of Organizations." *Administrative Science Quarterly* 6 (2): 129-166.

Clayton, Cornell W. 1999. "The Supreme Court in American Politics: New Institutionalist Interpretations." In *Supreme Court Decision-Making: New Instutionalist Approaches*, ed. Cornell W. Clayton and Howard Gillman. Chicago: University of Chicago Press, 15-41.

Clayton, Cornell W. and Howard Gillman, ed. 1999. *Supreme Court Decision-Making: New Instutionalist Approaches*. Chicago: University of Chicago Press.

Clinton, Robert Lowry. 1994. "Game Theory, Legal History, and the Origins of Judicial Review: A Revisionist Analysis of Marbury v. Madison." *American Journal of Political Science* 38 285-302.

Cohen, Donald. 1978. "Judicial Predictability in United States Supreme Court Oral Advocacy: Analysis of the Oral Argument in TVA v. Hill." *University of Puget Sound Law Review* 2 : 89-136.

Collins, Paul M., Jr. 2004. "Friends of the Court: Examining the Influence of Amicus Curiae Participation in U.S. Supreme Court Litigation." *Law and Society Review* 38 (4): 807–832.

Collins, Paul M., Jr. 2006. "Interest Group Influence on the Supreme Court: Theoretical and Methodological Considerations." Presented at the 77th Annual Meeting of the Southern Political Science Association, Atlanta, GA.

Collins, Paul M., Jr. 2007. "Lobbyists before the U.S. Supreme Court: Investigating the Influence of Amicus Curiae Briefs." *Political Research Quarterly* 60 (March): 55–70.

Collins, Paul M., Jr. 2008. *Friends of the Supreme Court: Interest Groups and Judicial Decision Making*. New York: Oxford University Press.

Collins, Paul M., Jr. and Lisa A. Solowiej. 2007. "Interest Group Participation, Competition, and Conflict in the U.S. Supreme Court." *Law and Social Inquiry*

Comparato, Scott A. 2003. *Amici Curiae and Strategic Behavior in State Supreme Courts*. N.p.: Praeger Publishers.

Comrey, Andrew L. and Howard B. Lee. 1992. *A First Course in Factor Analysis*. Second Edition. Hillsdale, NJ: Lawrence Erlbaum Associates.

Cooper, Joseph. 2001. "The Twentieth-Century Congress." In *Congress Reconsidered*, ed. Lawrence C. Dodd and Bruce I. Oppenheimer. Washington, D.C.: CQ Press, 335-366.

Corley, Pamela C. 2008. "The Supreme Court and Opinion Content: The Influence of Parties' Briefs." *Political Research Quarterly* 61 (September): 468-478.

Cortner, Richard C. 1968. "Strategies and Tactics of Litigants in Constitutional Cases." *Journal of Public Law* 17 (2): 287-307.

Cottrill, James, Terri Peretti, and Alan Rozzi. 2010. "The Partisan Dynamics of Supreme Court Confirmation Voting." Presented at the Annual Meeting of the American Political Science Association, Washington D.C.

Crawford, Vincent and Joel Sobel. 1982. "Strategic Information Transmission." *Econometrica* 60 (6): 1431-51.

Croley, Steven P. 1995. "The Majoritarian Difficulty: Elective Judiciaries and the Rule of Law." *The University of Chicago Law Review* 62 (2): 689–794.

Dahl, Robert A. 1993. "The Behavioral Approach in Political Science: Epitaph for a Monument to a Successful Protest." *American Political Science Review* 55 (1961): 763-772. Rpt. in *Discipline and History: Political Science in the United States*. Ed. Farr and Seidelman. 249-265.

Dahl, Robert. 1957. "Decisionmaking in a Democracy: The Supreme Court as a National Policymaker." *Journal of Public Law* 6 279-295.

Davidson, Roger H. and Walter J. Oleszek, ed. 2004. *Congress and Its Members*. Washington, D.C.: CQ Press.

Day, Jack G. 2001. "Words that Counted—A Vignette." *Case Western Reserve Law Review* 52 : 373–4.

Dean, Jodi. 2001. "Publicity's Secret." *Political Theory* 29 (October): 624-650.

Deen, Rebecca E., Joseph Igagni, and James Meernik. 2001. "Executive Influence on the U.S. Supreme Court: Solicitor General Amicus Cases, 1953–1997." *American Review of Politics* 22 (1): 3–26.

Deen, Rebecca E., Joseph Ignagni, and James Meernik. 2003. "The Solicitor General as Amicus, 1953–2000: How Influential?" *Judicature* 87 (2): 60–71.

Dodd, Lawrence C. and Bruce I. Oppenheimer, ed. 2001. *Congress Reconsidered.* Seventh Edition. Washington, D.C.: CQ Press.

Easton, David. 1993. "Political Science in the United States: Past and Present." *International Political Science Review* 6 (1985): 133-152. Rpt. in *Discipline and History: Political Science in the United States*. Ed. Farr and Seidelman. 291-309.

Elster, Jon, ed. 1998. *Deliberative Democracy*. New York: Cambridge University Press.

Ennis, Bruce J. 1984. "Symposium on Supreme Court Advocacy: Effective Amicus Briefs." *Catholic University Law Review* 33 (Spring): 603.

Eppler, Martin J. and Jeanne Mengis. 2004. "The Concept of Information Overload: A Review of Literature from Organization Science, Accounting, Marketing, MIS, and Related Disciplines." *The Information Society* 20 (5): 325–344.

Epstein, Lee and C. K. Rowland. 1991. "Debunking the Myth of Interest Group Invincibility in the Courts." *American Political Science Review* 85 (1): 205-217.

Epstein, Lee and Carol Mershon. 1996. "Measuring Political Preferences." *American Journal of Political Science* 40 (Feb.): 261-294.

Epstein, Lee and Jack Knight. 1995. "Documenting Strategic Interaction on the U.S. Supreme Court." Presented at the Annual Meeting of the American Political Science Association, Chicago.

Epstein, Lee and Jack Knight. 1998. *The Choices Justices Make*. Washington, D.C.: Congressional Quarterly, Inc.

Epstein, Lee and Jack Knight. 1999. "Mapping Out the Strategic Terrain: The Informational Role of Amici Curiae." In *Supreme Court Decision-Making: New Instutionalist Approaches*, ed. Cornell W. Clayton and Howard Gillman. Chicago: University of Chicago Press, 215-235.

Epstein, Lee and Jack Knight. 2000. "Toward a Strategic Revolution in Judicial Politics: A Look Back, A Look Ahead." *Political Research Quarterly* 53 (Sep.): 625-661.

Epstein, Lee and Jeffrey A. Segal. 2000. "Measuring Issue Salience." *American Journal of Political Science* 44 (1): 66-83.

Epstein, Lee and Joseph F. Kobylka. 1992. *The Supreme Court and Legal Change: Abortion and the Death Penalty*. Chapel Hill: University of North Carolina Press.

Epstein, Lee and Karen O'Connor. 1988. "States and the U.S. Supreme Court: An Examination of Litigation Outcomes." *Social Science Quarterly* 68 660–74.

Epstein, Lee, Jeffrey A. Segal, and Timothy Johnson. 1996. "The Claim of Issue Creation on the U.S. Supreme Court." *American Political Science Review* 90 (December): 845-852.

Epstein, Lee, Jeffrey A. Segal, Harold J. Spaeth, and Thomas G. Walker. 1996. *The Supreme Court Compendium: Data, Decisions, and Developments*. 2nd edition. Washington, D.C.: Congressional Quarterly Press.

Epstein, Lee, William M. Landes, Richard A. Posner. 2009. “Inferring the Winning Party in the Supreme Court from the Pattern of Questioning at Oral Argument.” University of Chicago Law & Economics, Olin Working Paper No. 466. Available at SSRN: http://ssrn.com/abstract=1414317.

Epstein, Lee, Valerie Hoekstra, Jeffrey A. Segal, and Harold J. Spaeth. 1998. "Do Political Preferences Change? A Longitudinal Study of U.S. Supreme Court Justices." *The Journal of Politics* 60 (Aug.): 801-818.

Epstein, Lee. 1991. "Courts and Interest Groups." In *The American Courts: A Critical Assessment*, ed. John B. Gates and Charles A. Johnson. Washington, D.C.: CQ Press, 335–371.

Epstein, Lee. 1993. "Interest Group Litigation During the Rehnquist Court Era." *Journal of Law and Politics* 9 639-717.

Epstein, Lee. 1995. *Contemplating Courts*. Washington, DC: Congressional Quarterly Books.

Eskridge, William N., Jr. 1991. "Overriding Supreme Court Satutory Interpretation Decisions." *Yale Law Journal* 101 331-417.

Eskridge, William N., Jr. 1991. "Reneging on History? Playing the Court/Congress/President Civil Rights Game." *California Law Review* 79 613-684.

Farber, Daniel A. and Philip P. Frickey. 1992. "Foreward: Positive Political Theory in the Nineties." *Georgetown Law Journal* 80 461.

Farganis, Dion, and Justin Wedeking. Forthcoming. " 'No Hints, No Forecasts, No Previews': An Empirical Analysis of Supreme Court Opinions." *Law and Society Review*.

Farganis, Dion, and Justin Wedeking. 2010. "Kagan's Candor: Updated Findings from the Recent Supreme Court Confirmation Hearings." Manuscript. Available at SSRN: http://ssrn.com/abstract=1628813.

Farganis, Dion. 2008. "Is the Supreme Court Bulletproof? Testing the Limits of Legitimacy with a New Experimental Design." Presented at the Annual Meeting of the Midwest Political Science Association, Chicago, IL.

Farr, James and Raymond Seidelman, ed. 1993. *Discipline and History: Political Science in the United States*. Ann Arbor, MI: University of Michigan Press.

Farrell, Joseph and Matthew Rabin. 1996. "Cheap Talk." *The Journal of Economic Perspectives* 10 (Summer): 103–118.

Farrell, Joseph and Robert Gibbons. 1989. "Cheap Talk with Two Audiences." *The American Economic Review* 79 (December): 1214–1223.

Farrell, Joseph. 1987. "Cheap Talk, Coordination, and Entry." *The RAND Journal of Economics* 18 (Spring): 34–39.

Feldman, Stephen M. 2008. "Do Supreme Court Nominees Lie? The Politics of Adjudication." *Southern California Interdisciplinary Law Journal* 18: 1-41.

Ferejohn, John and Barry Weingast. 1992. "A Positive Theory of Statutory Interpretation." *International Review of Law and Economics* 12 263.

Frey, Andrew. 2006. "Amici Curiae: Friends of the Court or Nuisances?" *Litigation* 33 (Fall): 5–9.

Friedman, Barry. 2000. "The History of the Countermajoritarian Difficulty, Part Four: Law's Politics." *University of Pennsylvania Law Review* 148 (4): 971–1064.

Friedman, Barry. 2002. "The Birth of an Academic Obsession: The History of the Countermajoritarian Difficulty, Part 5"." *The Yale Law Journal* 112 (2): 153–259.

Friedman, Barry. 2006. "Taking Law Seriously." *Perspectives on Politics* 4 (June): 261–276.

Funston, Richard. 1975. "The Supreme Court and Critical Elections." *The American Political Science Review* 69 (September): 795-811.

Galanter, Marc. 1974. "Why the 'Haves' Come out Ahead: Speculations on the Limits of Legal Change." *Law & Society Review* 9 95–160.

Galloway, Russell. 1989. "Oral Argument in the Court." *Trial* 25 78-84.

Garcia, Ruben J. 2008. "A Democratic Theory of Amicus Government." *Florida State University Law Review* 35 : 315–58.

Gates, John B. 1998. "The Motivations for Interest Group Litigation in a Changing Interest Group Environment." University of California, Davis. Manuscript.

Gates, John B. and Charles A. Johnson, ed. 1991. *The American Courts: A Critical Assessment*. Washington, D.C.: CQ Press.

George, Tracey E. and Lee Epstein. 1992. "On the Nature of Supreme Court Decision Making." *American Political Science Review* 86 325.

Gibson, James. 1997. "United States Supreme Court Judicial Database: Phase II." Produced by University of Houston: Houston, TX. Distributed by ICPSR: Ann Arbor, MI.

Gillman, Howard and Cornell Clayton, ed. 1999. *The Supreme Court in American Politics: New Institutionalist Interpretations*. Lawrence, KS: University Press of Kansas.

Gillman, Howard. 1997. "Placing Judicial Motives in Context." *Law and Courts* 7 10-13.

Gillman, Howard. 2003. "Separating the Wheat from the Chaff in The Supreme Court and the Attitudinal Model Revisited." *Law and Courts Newsletter* 13 (Summer): 12–18.

Goldman, Brian P. 2011. "Should the Supreme Court Stop Inviting *Amici Curiae* to Defend Abandoned Lower Court Decisions?" *Stanford Law Review* 63 (April): 907-972.

Greenhouse, Linda. 2004. "Press Room Predictions." *Perspectives on Politics* 2 (December): 781–784.

Gutmann, Amy and Dennis Thompson. 2004. *Why Deliberative Democracy?* Princeton, NJ: Princeton University Press.

Hagle, Timothy M. 1991. "But Do They Have to See It to Know It? The Supreme Court's Obscenity and Pornography Decision." *The Western Political Quarterly* 44 (December): 1039–1054.

Hagle, Timothy M. and Harold J. Spaeth. 1991. "Voting Fluidity and the Attitudinal Model of Supreme Court Decision Making." *The Western Political Quarterly* 44 (Mar.): 119-128.

Haider, Donald H. 1974. *When Governments Come to Washington: Governors, Mayors, and Intergovernmental Lobbying*. N.p.: Simon .

Halpern, Stephen C. 1976. "Assessing the Litigative Role of ACLU Chapters." In *Civil Liberties: Policy and Policy Making*, ed. Stephen L. Wasby. Lexington, MA: Lexington Books, np.

Hammond, Thomas H., Chris W. Bonneau, and Reginald S. Sheehan. 2005. *Strategic Behavior and Policy Choice on the U.S. Supreme Court*. Stanford, CA: Stanford University Press.

Hansford, Thomas G. and David F. Damore. 2000. "Congressional Preferences, Perceptions of Threat, and Supreme Court Decision Making." *American Politics Quarterly* 28 (4): 490-510.

Hansford, Thomas G. and James F. Spriggs II. 2006. *The Politics of Precedent on the U.S. Supreme Court*. Princeton, NJ: Princeton University Press.

Hansford, Thomas. 2004. "Information Provision, Organizational Constraints, and the Decision to Submit an Amicus Curiae Brief in a U.S. Supreme Court Case." *Political Research Quarterly* 57 (June): 219-230.

Harlan, John. 1955. "What Part Does the Oral Argument Play in The Conduct of an Appeal." *Cornell Law Quarterly* 41 : 6.

Harris, John F. 2005. "In Recent Scandals, a Rethinking of Capital's Conventional Wisdom." *Washington Post* April 12: A01.

Heberlig, Eric S. and Rorie L. Spill. 2000. "Congress at Court: Members of Congress as Amicus Curiae." *Southeastern Political Review* 189

Hoekstra, Valerie and Timothy R. Johnson. 2003. "Delaying Justice: The Supreme Court's Decision to Hear Rearguments." *Political Research Quarterly* 56 (Sep.): 351-360.

Hojnacki, Marie and David C. Kimball. 1998. "Organized Interests and the Decision of Whom to Lobby in Congress." *American Political Science Review* 92 (4): 775-790.

Howard, J. Woodford. 1968. "On the Fluidity of Judicial Choice." *American Political Science Review* 62 43-56.

Idleman, Scott C. 2005. "The Concealment of Religious Values in Judicial Decisionmaking." *Virginia Law Review* 91 (April): 515–534.

Ignagni, Joseph and James Meernik. 1994. "Explaining Congressional Attempts to Reverse Supreme Court Decisions." *Political Research Quarterly* 47 353-371.

Irish, Marian D., ed. 1968. *Political Science: Advance of a Discipline*. Englewood Cliffs, NJ: Prentice-Hall.

Ivers, Gregg. 1992. "Religious Organizations as Constitutional Litigants." *Polity* 25 (Winter): 243–266.

Jackson, Robert H. 1951. "Advocacy Before the United States Supreme Court." *Cornell Law Quarterly* 37 (Fall): 1–16.

Johnson, Charles A. and John B. Gates, ed. 1990. *The American Courts: A Critical Assessment*. Washington, DC: CQ Press.

Johnson, Timothy R. 2001. "Information, Oral Arguments, and Supreme Court Decision Making." *American Politics Research* 29 (4): 331-351.

Johnson, Timothy R. 2003. "The Supreme Court, The Solicitor General, and the Separation of Powers." *American Politics Research* 31 (July): 426–451.

Johnson, Timothy R. 2004. *Oral Arguments and Decision Making on the United States Supreme Court*. SUNY Series in American Constitutionalism. Ed. Robert J. Spitzer. Albany, NY: State University of New York Press.

Johnson, Timothy R. and Andrew D. Martin. 1998. "The Public's Conditional Response to Supreme Court Decisions." *The American Political Science Review* 92 (Jun.): 299-309.

Johnson, Timothy R. and Matthew M.C. Roberts. 2004. "Amicus Curiae: the Informational Role of Supreme Court Oral Arguments." Presented at the Annual Meeting of the Midwest Political Science Association, Chicago, IL.

Johnson, Timothy R., James F. Spriggs II, and Paul J. Wahlbeck. 2007. "Supreme Court Oral Advocacy: Does it affect the Justices' Decisions?" *Washington University Law Review* 85 : 457–527.

Johnson, Timothy R., Paul J. Wahlbeck, and James F. Spriggs II. 2006. "The Influence of Oral Arguments on the U.S. Supreme Court." *American Political Science Review* 100 (February): 99–113.

Johnson, Timothy R., Ryan Black, Jerry Goldman, and Sarah Treul. 2009. "Inquiring Minds Want to Know: Do Justices Tip their Hands with Questions at Oral Argument in the U.S. Supreme Court?" *Washington University Journal of Law and Policy* 29 (1): 241-261.

Johnson, Timothy R., Ryan C. Black, and Justin P. Wedeking. 2008. "Oral Arguments and the Process of Coalition Formation on the U.S. Supreme Court." Presented at the Annual Meeting of the American Political Science Association, Boston, MA.

Johnson, Timothy R., Ryan C. Black, and Justin Wedeking. 2009. "Pardon the Interruption: An Empirical Analysis of Supreme Court Justices' Behavior During Oral Arguments." *Loyola Law Review* 55: 331-351.

Johnson, Timothy, Ryan Black, and Sarah Treul. 2009. "Jekyll and Hyde Questions from the Bench: Does the Emotional Nature of Justices' Questions Affect their Votes on the Merits?" Presented at the 67th Annual National Conference of the Midwest Political Science Association, Chicago, IL.

Kassop, Nancy. 1993. "From Arguments to Supreme Court Opinions in Planned Parenthood v. Casey." *PS: Political Science and Politics* 26 (Mar.): 53-58.

Kastellec, Jonathan P., Jeffrey R. Lax, and Justin Phillips. 2010. "Public Opinion and Senate Confirmation of Supreme Court Nominees." *Journal of Politics* 72 (3): 767-784.

Kearney, Joseph D. and Thomas W. Merrill. 2000. "The Influence of Amicus Curiae Briefs on the Supreme Court." *University of Pennsylvania Law Review* 148 (3): 743-855.

King, Gary and Langche Zeng. 2001. "Logistic Regression in Rare Events Data." *Political Analysis* 9 (2): 137-163.

King, Gary, Michael Tomz, and Jason Wittenberg. 2000. "Making the Most of Statistical Analyses: Improving Interpretation and Presentation." *American Journal of Political Science* 44 (2): 347-61.

Knight, Jack and Lee Epstein. 1996. "The Norm of Stare Decisis." *American Journal of Political Science* 40 (Nov.): 1018-1035.

Kolbert, Kathryn. 1989. "The Webster Amicus Curiae Briefs: Perspectives on the Abortion Controversy and the Role of the Supreme Court." *American Journal of Law and Medicine* 15 153–168.

Koshansky, Joseph, Jr. 1977. "The Amicus Curiae and Supreme Court Decision-making." Mast. Thesis. The University of Tennessee at Knoxville.

Krehbiel, Keith. 2007. "Supreme Court Appointments as a Move-the-Median Game." *American Journal of Political Science* 51 (2): 231-240.

Krippendorff, K. 1980. *Content Analysis: An Introduction to Its Methodology*. Newbury Park, CA: Sage.

Krislov, Samuel. 1963. "The Amicus Curiae Brief: From Friendship to Advocacy." *The Yale Law Journal* 72 (Mar.): 694-721.

Kucinski, Nancy Ellis. 2004. "Interests, Institutions, and Friends of the Court: An Analysis of Organizational Factors Related to Amicus Curiae Participation." Ph.D. diss. University of Texas at Dallas.

Kurland, Philip B. 1969. "Toward a Political Supreme Court." *University of Chicago Law Review* 37: 19.

Lane, Charles. 2003. "Court Hears Arguments on Ky. HMO Law." *Washington Post* January 15: A06.

Lane, Charles. 2003. "High Court Considers Cost of Prescriptions Justices Appear Hesitant to Make Political, Economic Tradeoffs in Maine Case." *Washington Post* January 23: A02.

Lanier, Drew Noble. 2003. *Of Time and Judicial Behavior: United States Supreme Court Agenda-Setting and Decision-Making, 1888-1997*. Selinsgrove, PA: Susquehanna University Press.

Lazarus, Richard J. 2008. "Advocacy Matters Before and Within the Supreme Court: Transforming the Court by Transforming the Bar." *The Georgetown Law Journal* 96: 1487-1564.

Li, Hao and Suen Wing. 2004. "Delegating Decisions to Experts." *Journal of Political Economy* 112 311–335.

Liptak, Adam. 2010. "Court Under Roberts Is Most Conservative in Decades." *The New York Times*, July 24: A1.

Lynch, Kelly J. 2004. "Best Friends? Supreme Court Law Clerks on Effective Amicus Curiae Briefs." *Journal of Law and Politics* 20 (33): 33–73.

Maltzman, Forest, James F. Spriggs II, and Paul J. Wahlbeck. 1999. "Strategy and Judicial Choice: New Institutionalist Approaches to Supreme Court Decision-Making." In *Supreme Court Decision-Making: New Instutionalist Approaches*, ed. Cornell W. Clayton and Howard Gillman. Chicago: University of Chicago Press, 43-63.

Maltzman, Forrest and Paul J. Wahlbeck. 1996. "May It Please the Chief? Opinion Assignments in the Rehnquist Court." *American Journal of Political Science* 40 421-443.

Maltzman, Forrest and Paul J. Wahlbeck. 1996. "Strategic Considerations and Vote Fluidity on the Burger Court." *American Political Science Review* 90 (Sep.): 581-592.

Maltzman, Forrest and Paul J. Wahlbeck. 2004. "A Conditional Model of Opinion Assignment on the Supreme Court." *Political Research Quarterly* 57 (December): 551–563.

Maltzman, Forrest, James F. Spriggs II, and Paul J. Wahlbeck. 2000. *Crafting Law on the Supreme Court: The Collegial Game*. New York: Cambridge University Press.

Manelli, Alejandro M. 1996. "Cheap Talk and Sequential Equilibria in Signaling Games." *Econometrica* 64 (July): 917–942.

Marek, Lynne. 2006. "Exacting Easterbrook to Be Chief of 7th Circuit." *The National Law Journal*. August 29, 2006. http://www.law.com/jsp/article.jsp?id=1156769031655 (June 24, 2008).

Marshall, Thomas. 1989. *Public Opinion and the Supreme Court*. New York: Longman.

Martin, Andrew and Kevin Quinn. 2002. "Dynamic Ideal Point Estimation via Markov Chain Monte Carlo for the U.S. Supreme Court, 1953-1999." *Political Analysis* 10 (2): 134-53.

Martin, Andrew D. and Kevin M. Quinn. 2002. "Dynamic Ideal Point Estimation via Markov Chain Monte Carlo for the U.S. Supreme Court, 1953–1999." *Political Analysis* 10 134–153.

Martinek, Wendy L. 2006. "Amici Curiae in the U.S. Courts of Appeals." *American Politcs Research* 34 (November): 803–824.

Mather, Lynn. 1995. "The Fired Football Coach (Or, How Trial Courts Make Policy)." In *Contemplating Courts*, Washington, DC: Congressional Quarterly Books, 170-202.

McAtee, Andrea and Kevin T. McGuire. 2007. "Lawyers, Justices, and Issue Salience: When and How do Legal Arguments Affect the U.S. Supreme Court?" *Law & Society Review* 41 (2): 259-278.

McCann, Michael. 1999. "How the Supreme Court Matters in American Politics: New Institutionalist Perspectives." In *The Supreme Court in American Politics: New Institutionalist Interpretations*, ed. Howard Gillman and Cornell Clayton. Lawrence, KS: University Press of Kansas, 63-97.

McFeeley, Neil and Richard Ault. 1979. "Supreme Court Oral Argument." *Jurimetrics Journal* 20 52-83.

McGuire, Kevin T. 1990. "Obscenity, Libertarian Values, and Decision Making in the Supreme Court." *American Politics Quarterly* 18 (1): 47-67.

McGuire, Kevin T. 1993. "Lawyers and the U.S. Supreme Court: The Washington Community and Legal Elites." *American Journal of Political Science* 37 (May): 365–390.

McGuire, Kevin T. 1994. "Amici Curiae and Strategies for Gaining Access to the Supreme Court." *Political Research Quarterly* 47 (December): 821-837.

McGuire, Kevin T. 1995. "Repeat Players in the Supreme Court: The Role of Experienced Lawyers in Litigation Success." *Journal of Politics* 57 (1): 187-196.

McGuire, Kevin T. 1998. "Explaining Executive Success in the U.S. Supreme Court." *Political Research Quarterly* 51 (2): 505–526.

McGuire, Kevin T. 2002. *Understanding the U.S. Supreme Court: Cases and Controversies*. New York: McGraw Hill.

McGuire, Kevin T. and Barbara Palmer. 1995. "Issue Fluidity on the U.S. Supreme Court." *American Political Science Review* 89 691–702.

McGuire, Kevin T. and Gregory A. Caldeira. 1993. "Lawyers, Organized Interests, and the Law of Obscenity: Agenda Setting in the Supreme Court." *The American Political Science Review* 87 (September): 717–726.

McGuire, Kevin T. and James A. Stimson. 2004. "The Least Dangerous Branch Revisited: New Evidence on Supreme Court Responsiveness to Public Preferences." *The Journal of Politics* 66 (November): 1018–1035.

McLauchlan, Judithanne Scourfield. 2005. *Congressional Participation as Amicus Curiae Before the U.S. Supreme Court*. New York: LFP Scholarly Publishing.

Meinhold, Stephen S. and Steven A. Shull. 1998. "Policy Congruence between the President and the Solicitor General." *Political Research Quarterly* 51 (June): 527–537.

Merrill, Thomas W. 1998. "High-Level, 'Tenured' Lawyers." *Law and Contemporary Problems* 61 (Spring): 83–108.

Milbrath, Lester W. 1963. *The Washington Lobbyists*. Chicago: Rand McNally.

Mishler, William and Reginald S. Sheehan. 1993. "The Supreme Court as a Countermajoritarian Institution? The Impact of Public Opinion on Supreme Court Decisions." *The American Political Science Review* 87 (March): 87-101.

Moe, Terry M. 1980. *The Organization of Interests: Incentives and the Internal Dynamics of Political Interest Groups*. Chicago: University of Chicago Press.

Mooney, Christopher and Robert D. Duval. 1993. *Bootstrapping: A Nonparametric Approach to Statistical Inference*. Newbury Park, CA: Sage.

Morris, Thomas. 1987. "States before the U.S. Supreme Court: State attorneys general as amicus curiae." *Judicature* 70 (5): 298-305.

Mulier, Vincent. 2006. "Recognizing the Full Scope of the Right to Take Fish Under the Stevens Treaties: The History of Fishing Rights Litigation in the Pacific Northwest." *American Indian Law Review* 31

Munford, Luther T. 1999. "When Does the Curiae Need an Amicus?" *The Journal of Appellate Practice and Process* 1 279–294.

Nelson, Forrest and Lawrence Olson. 1978. "Specification and Estimation of a Simultaneous-Equation Model with Limited Dependent Variables." *International Economic Review* 19 (3): 695-709.

Nicholson, Chris and Paul M. Collins Jr. 2007. "Selecting Influence? The Solicitor General and the Supreme Court." Presented at the Annual Meeting of the Midwest Political Science Association, Chicago, IL.

Nicholson, Chris and Paul M. Collins Jr. 2008. "The Solicitor General's Amicus Curiae Strategies in the Supreme Court." *American Politics Research* 36 (May): 382–415.

Nicholson, Chris. 2009. "State Attorneys General and their Amicus Curiae Strategies Before the Supreme Court: 1946–1971." Presented at the Annual Meeting of the Southern Political Science Association, New Orleans, LA.

Nicholson, Stephen P. and Robert M. Howard. 2003. "Framing Support for the Supreme Court in the Aftermath of 'Bush v Gore'." *The Journal of Politics* 65 (August): 676–695.

O'Connor, Karen and Lee Epstein. 1983. "Court Rules and Workload: A Case Study of Rules Governing Amicus Curiae Participation." *The Justice System Journal* 8 (Spring): 35–45.

O'Connor, Karen. 1983. "The Amicus Curiae Role of the U.S. Solicitor General in Supreme Court Litigation." *Judicature* 66 (December-January): 256-64.

O'Connor, Karen. 1983. "The Amicus Curiae Role of the U.S. Solicitor General in Supreme Court Litigation." *Judicature* 66 256.

Olson, Susan M. 1990. "Interest-Group Litigation in Federal District Court: Beyond the Political Disadvantage Theory." *Journal of Politics* 52 (3): 854-882.

Ordeshook, Peter C. 1986. *Game Theory and Political Theory: An Introduction.* Cambridge: Cambridge University Press.

Ornstein, Norman J. and Amy L. Schenkenberg. 1995. "Congress Bashing: External Pressures for Reform and the Future of the Institution." In *Remaking Congress: Change and Stability in the 1990s*, ed. James A. Thurber and Roger H. Davidson. Washington, D.C.: Congressional Quarterly Books, 116-129.

Osborne, Martin J. 2003. *An Introduction to Game Theory.* N.p.: Oxford University Press.

Owens, Ryan J. and Lee Epstein. 2005. "Amici Curiae during the Rehnquist Years." *Judicature* 89 (November-December): 127–132.

Pacelle, Richard L., Jr. 2006. "Amicus curiae or amicus praesidentis? Reexamining the role of the solicitor general in filing amici." *Judicature* 89 (May-June): 317–325.

Pacelle, Richard. 2001. *The Supreme Court in American Politics: The Least Dangerous Branch.* N.p.: Westview Press.

Palmer, Jan. 1982. "An Econometric Analysis of the U.S. Supreme Court's Certiorari ." *Public Choice* 39 387.

Peppers, Todd C. 2006. *Courtiers of the Marble Palace: The Rise and Influence of the Supreme Court Law Clerk.* Stanford, CA: Stanford University Press.

Peretti, Terri. 2008. "Constructing Courts in Polarized Times." Presented at the "Going to Extremes" conference, Dartmouth College. Available at SSRN: http://ssrn.com/abstract=1307789.

Perry, H.W., Jr. 1991. *Deciding to Decide: Agenda Setting in the United States Supreme Court*. Cambridge, MA: Harvard University Press.

Pfeffer, Leo. 1981. "Amici in Church-State Litigation." *Law and Contemporary Problems* 44 (Spring): 83–110.

Phillips, James C. and Edward L. Carter. 2009a. "Gender and U. S. Supreme Court Oral Argument on the Roberts Court: An Empirical Examination of the Sotomayor Hypothesis." Manuscript. Available at SSRN: http://ssrn.com/abstract=1483330.

Phillips, James C. and Edward L. Carter. 2009b. "Oral Argument in the Roberts Court: A Qualitative and Quantitative Analysis of Individual Justice Behavior." Manuscript. Available at SSRN: http://ssrn.com/abstract=1472489.

Phillips, James C. and Ed L. Carter. 2009c. "Source of Information or Dog and Pony Show: Information Seeking During Oral Argument in the U.S. Supreme Court, 1960s & 2000s." Presented at the 67th Annual National Conference of the Midwest Political Science Association, Chicago, IL.

Phillips, James C. and Edward L. Carter. 2009d. "Source of Information or 'Dog and Pony Show'? Judicial Information Seeking During U.S. Supreme Court Oral Argument, 1963-65 & 2004-09." *Santa Clara Law Review* 50.

Pickerill, J. Mitchell and Cornell W. Clayon. 2004. "The Rehnquist Court and the Political Dynamics of Federalism." *Perspectives on Politics* 2 (June): 233-48.

Pika, Joseph A. and John Anthony Maltese. 2004. *The Politics of the Presidency*. Washington, D.C.: CQ Press.

Plutchik, Robert and Henry Kellerman, ed. 1989. *Theory, Research, and Experience*. New York: Academic Press.

Poole, Keith T. 1998. "Recovering a Base Space from a Set of Issue Scales." *American Journal of Political Science* 42 (July): 954-993.

Poundstone, William. 2008. *Gaming the Vote: Why Elections Aren't Fair (and What We Can Do About It)*. New York: Hill and Wang.

Prettyman, . 1978. "Supreme Court Advocacy: Random Thoughts in a Day of Time Restrictions." *Litigation* 4 (Winter).

Prettyman, E. Barrett, Jr. 1984. "The Supreme Court's Use of Hypothetical Questions at Oral Argument." *Catholic University Law Review* 33 (Spring): 555.

Pritchett, C. Herman. 1968. "Public Law and Judicial Behavior." In *Political Science: Advance of a Discipline*, ed. Marian D. Irish. Englewood Cliffs, NJ: Prentice-Hall, 190-219.

Project, The Oyez. 1980. "McLain v. Real Estate Board of New Orleans, 444 U.S. 232." http://oyez.org/cases/1970-1979/1979/1979_78_1501 (Tuesday, April 28, 2009).

Project, The Oyez. 1980. "Schaumburg v. Citizens for a Better Environment, 444 U.S. 620." http://oyez.org/cases/1970-1979/1979/1979_78_1335 (Tuesday, April 28, 2009).

Provine, Doris Marie. 1980. *Case Selection in the United States Supreme Court*. Chicago: University of Chicago Press.

Puro, Steven. 1971. "The Role of Amicus Curiae in the United States Supreme Court: 1920–1966." Ph.D. Dissertation. Department of Political Science, State University of New York at Buffalo.

Puro, Steven. 1981. "The United States as Amicus Curiae." In *Courts, Law and Judicial Processes*, ed. S. Sidney Ulmer. New York: The Free Press, np.

Rehnquist, William H. 1984. "Oral Advocacy: A Disappearing Art." *Mercer Law Review* 34 : 1015-1028.

Rehnquist, William H. 2002. *The Supreme Court*. New York: Vintage Books-Random House, Inc.

Rieselbach, Leroy N. 1995. "Congressional Change: Historical Perspectives." In *Remaking Congress: Change and Stability in the 1990s*, ed. James A. Thurber and Roger H. Davidson. Washington, D.C.: Congressional Quarterly Books, 9-27.

Roberts, John G., Jr. 2005. "Oral Advocacy and the Re-emergence of a Supreme Court Bar." *Journal of Supreme Court History* 30 (1): 68–81.

Rodriguez, Daniel B. 1994. "The Positive Political Dimensions of Regulatory Reform." *Washington University Law Quarterly* 72 1-150.

Roesch, Ronald, Stephen L. Golding V, alerie P. Hans, and N. Dickon Reppucci. 1991. "Social Science and the Courts: The Role of Amicus Curiae Briefs." *Law and Human Behavior* 15 (February): 1–11.

Rogers, James R. 2001. "Information and Judicial Review: A Signalling Game of Legislative-Judicial Interaction." *American Journal of Political Science* 45 (January): 84-99.

Rohde, David W. 1972. "Policy Goals and Opinion Coalitions in the Supreme Court." *Midwest Journal of Political Science* 16 208-224.

Rohde, David W. and Kenneth A. Shepsle. 2007. "Advising and Consenting in the 60-Vote Senate: Strategic Appointments to the Supreme Court." *The Journal of Politics* 69 (August): 664-677.

Rohde, David W. and Harold Spaeth. 1976. *Supreme Court Decision Making*. Gordonsville, VA: W H Freeman.

Rosenberg, Gerald N. 1993. *The Hollow Hope: Can Courts Bring About Social Change?* Chicago: University of Chicago Press.

Rosenberg, Gerald N. 1994. "Symposium: The Supreme Court and the Attitudinal Model." *Law and Courts* 4 (Spring): 6-8.

Rosenblum, Victor G. 1955. *Law as a Political Instrument*. New York: Doubleday.

Ruckman, P.S., Jr. 1993. "The Supreme Court, Critical Nominations, and the Senate Confirmation Process." *The Journal of Politics* 55 (August): 793-805.

Sala, Brian R. and James F. Spriggs II. 2004. "Designing Tests of the Supreme Court and the Separation of Powers." *Political Research Quarterly* 57 (June): 197–208.

Salisbury, Robert H. 1984. "Interest Representation: The Dominance of Institutions." *American Political Science Review* 78 (1): 64-76.

Salokar, Rebecca M. 1992. *The Solicitor General: The Politics of Law*. Philadelphia: Temple University.

Samuels, Suzanne U. 2004. *First among friends: Interest groups, the U.S. Supreme Court, and the Right to Privacy*. Westport, CT: Praeger.

Scheppele, Kim Lane and Jack L. Walker Jr. 1991. "The Litigation Strategies of Interest Groups." In *Mobilizing Interest Groups in America*, ed. Jack L. Walker Jr. Ann Arbor: University of Michigan Press, np.

Schlozman, Kay Lehman and John T. Tierney. 1986. *Organized Interests and American Democracy*. New York: Harper & Row.

Schmidt, Patrick D. and David A. Yalof. 2004. "The 'Swing Voter' Revisited: Justice Anthony Kennedy and the First Amendment Right of Free Speech." *Political Research Quarterly* 57 (June): 209-217.

Schubert, Glendon, ed. 1963. *Judicial Decision Making*. New York: Free Press.

Schubert, Glendon. 1958. "The Study of Judicial Decision-Making as An Aspect of Political Behavior." *American Political Science Review* 52 1007-1025.

Schubert, Glendon. 1959. *Quantitative Analysis of Judicial Behavior*. Glencoe, IL: Free Press.

Schubert, Glendon. 1997. "Oral Argument in Supreme Court Decision Making: Ethological and Paralinguistic Analysis of Psychophysiological Biosocial Political Behavior." In *Recent Explorations in Biology and Politics*, ed. Albert Somit and Steven A. Peterson. Greenwich, CT: Jai Press, 3–56.

Schubert, James N., Steven A. Peterson, Glendon Schubert, and Stephen Wasby. 1992. "Observing Supreme Court oral argument: A Biosocial Approach." *Politcs and the Life Sciences* 11 (February): 35–51.

Schubert, James N., Steven Peterson, Glendon A. Schubert, and Stephen L. Wasby. 1990. "Studying Supreme Court Oral Argument." Presented at the Annual Meeting of the American Political Science Association, San Francisco.

Schubert, James N., Steven Peterson, Glendon A. Schubert, and Stephen L. Wasby. 1991a. "Judicial Involvement and Leadership in Oral Argument." Presented at the meeting of the International Society for Political Psychology, Helsinki.

Schubert, James N., Steven Peterson, Glendon A. Schubert, and Stephen L. Wasby. 1991b. "Dissensus and Unanimity in Supreme Court Decision Making." Presented at the meeting of the International Political Science Association, Buenos Aires.

Schwartz, Edward P. 1992. "Policy, Precedent, and Power: A Positive Theory of Supreme Court Decision Making." *Journal of Law, Economics, and Organizations* 8 219-252.

Schwarz, Gideon. 1978. "Estimating the Dimension of a Model." *The Annals of Statistics* 6 (March): 461–464.

Scigliano, Robert. 1971. *The Supreme Court and the Presidency*. New York: Free Press.

Scott, Kevin M. and Wendy L. Martinek. 2009. "Judicial Selection & Judicial Choice." Presented at the Annual Meeting of the American Political Science Association, Toronto.

Segal, Jeffrey A. 1988. "Amicus Curiae Briefs by the Solicitor General During the Warren and Burger Courts: A Research Note." *Western Political Quarterly* 41 (March): 135–144.

Segal, Jeffrey A. 1997. "Separation-of-Powers Games in the Positive Theory of Congress and Courts." *American Political Science Review* 91 28-44.

Segal, Jeffrey A. and Albert D. Cover. 1989. "Ideological Values and the Votes of U.S. Supreme Court Justices." *The American Political Science Review* 83 (Jun.): 557-565.

Segal, Jeffrey A. and Cheryl D. Reedy. 1988. "The Supreme Court and Sex Discrimination: The Role of the Solicitor General." *Western Political Quarterly* 41 (September): 553–568.

Segal, Jeffrey A. and Harold J. Spaeth. 1993. *The Supreme Court and the Attitudinal Model.* New York: Cambridge University Press.

Segal, Jeffrey A. and Harold J. Spaeth. 1996. "Norms, Dragons, and Stare Decisis: A Response." *American Journal of Political Science* 40 (Nov.): 1064-1082.

Segal, Jeffrey A. and Harold J. Spaeth. 1996. "The Influence of Stare Decisis on the Votes of United States Supreme Court Justices." *American Journal of Political Science* 40 (Nov.): 971-1003.

Segal, Jeffrey A. and Harold J. Spaeth. 2002. *The Supreme Court and the Attitudinal Model Revisited.* New York: Cambridge University Press.

Segal, Jeffrey A., Charles M. Cameron, and Albert D. Cover. 1992. "Spatial Model of Roll Call Voting: Senators, Constituents, Presidents, and Interest Groups in Supreme Court Confirmations." *American Journal of Political Science* 36 (Feb.): 96-121.

Segal, Jeffrey A., Lee Epstein, Charles M. Cameron, and Harold J. Spaeth. 1995. "Ideological Values and the Votes of U.S. Supreme Court Justices Revisited." *The Journal of Politics* 57 (Aug.): 812-823.

Shapiro, Ilya. 2008. "Friends of the Second Amendment: A Walk through the Amicus Briefs in *D.C. v. Heller*." Journal on Firearms and Public Policy 20: 15-41.

Shapiro, Martin. 1964. *Law and Politics in the Supreme Court.* New York: Free Press.

Shapiro, Martin. 1986. *Courts: A Comparative and Political Analysis.* Chicago: University of Chicago Press.

Shapiro, Stephen M. 1984. "Oral Argument in the Supreme Court of the United States." *Catholic University Law Review* 33 (Spring): 529.

Sheehan, Reginald S., William Mishler, and Donald R. Songer. 1992. "Ideology, Status, and the Differential Success of Direct Parties Before the Supreme Court." *The American Political Science Review* 86 (June): 464–471.

Shullman, Sarah Levien. 2004. "The Illusion of Devil's Advocacy: How the Justices of the Supreme Court Foreshadow Their Decisions During Oral Argument." 6: 271.

Simmons, Omari Scott. 2009. "Picking Friends From the Crowd: Amicus Participation as Political Symbolism." *Connecticut Law Review* 42: 185-233.

Slotnick, Elliot E. and Jennifer A. Segal. 1998. *Television News and the Supreme Court: All the News that's Fit to Air?* New York: Cambridge University Press.

Smith, Christopher E. 1993. *Courts, Politics, and the Judicial Process.* Chicago: Nelson-Hall Press.

Somit, Albert and Joseph Tanenhaus. 1967. *The Development of American Political Science: from Burgess to behavioralism.* Boston: Allyn and Bacon.

Somit, Albert and Steven A. Peterson, ed. 1997. *Recent Explorations in Biology and Politics*. Greenwich, CT: Jai Press.

Songer, Donald R. and Reginald S. Sheehan. 1992. "Upperdogs and Underdogs in the United States Courts of Appeals." *American Journal of Political Science* 36 (February): 235–258.

Songer, Donald R. and Reginald S. Sheehan. 1993. "Interest Group Success in the Courts: Amicus Participation in the Supreme Court." *Political Research Quarterly* 46 (July): 339-354.

Songer, Donald R. and Sefanie A. Lindquist. 1996. "Not the Whole Story: The Impact of Justices' Values on Supreme Court Decision Making." *American Journal of Political Science* 40 (Nov.): 1049-1063.

Songer, Donald R., Jeffrey A. Segal, and Charles M. Cameron. 1994. "The Hierarchy of Justice: Testing a Principal-Agent Model of Supreme Court-Circuit Court Interactions." *American Journal of Political Science* 38 (August): 673-696.

Songer, Donald, Ashlyn Kuersten, and Erin Kaheny. 2000. "Why the Haves Don't Always Come out Ahead: Repeat Players Meet Amici Curiae for the Disadvantaged." *Political Research Quarterly* 53 (September): 537–556.

Spaeth, Harold J. 1961. "An Approach to the Study of Attitudinal Differences as an Aspect of Judicial Behavior." *Midwest Journal of Political Science* 5 (May): 165-180.

Spaeth, Harold J. 1962. "Judicial Power as a Variable Motivating Supreme Court Behavior." *Midwest Journal of Political Science* 6 (Feb.): 54-82.

Spaeth, Harold J. 1964. "The Judicial Restraint of Mr. Justice Frankfurter--Myth or Reality." *Midwest Journal of Political Science* 8 (Feb.): 22-38.

Spaeth, Harold J. 1965. "Jurimetrics and Professor Mendelson: A Troubled Relationship." *The Journal of Politics* 27 (Nov.): 875-880.

Spaeth, Harold J. 1972. *An Introduction to Supreme Court Decision Making.* Revised Edition. San Francisco: Chandler Publishing Company.

Spaeth, Harold J. 1979. *Supreme Court Policy Making: Explanation and Prediction.* San Francisco: W. H. Freeman and Company.

Spaeth, Harold J. 2001. "United States Supreme Court Judicial Database, 1953–2000 Terms." Distributed by Michigan State University: East Lansing, MI.

Spaeth, Harold J. and Jeffrey A. Segal. 1989. "Decisional Trends on the Warren and Burger Court: Results from the Supreme Court Data Base Project." *Judicature* 72 103-107.

Spaeth, Harold J. and Jeffrey A. Segal. 1999. *Majority Rule or Minority Will: Adherence to Precedent on the U.S. Supreme Court.* New York: Cambridge University Press.

Spiller, Pablo T. and Emerson H. Tiller. 1996. "Invitations to Override: Congressional Reversals of Supreme Court Decisions." *International Review of Law and Economics* 16 503-521.

Spiller, Pablo T. and Rafael Gely. 1992. "Congressional Control of Judicial Independence: The Determinants of U.S. Supreme Court Labor-Relations Decisions, 1949-1988." *RAND Journal of Economics* 23 463-492.

Spriggs, James F. and Paul J. Wahlbeck. 1997. "Amicus Curiae and the Role of Information at the Supreme Court." *Political Science Quarterly* 50 (June): 365-86.

Spriggs, James F., II and Thomas G. Hansford. 2001. "Explaining the Overruling of U.S. Supreme Court Precedent." *The Journal of Politics* 63 (Nov.): 1091-1111.

Spriggs, James F., II, Forrest Maltzman, and Paul J. Wahlbeck. 1999. "Bargaining on the U.S. Supreme Court: Justices' Responses to Majority Opinion Drafts." *The Journal of Politics* 61 (May): 485-506.

Stern, Robert L., Eugene Gressman, Stephen M. Shapiro, and Kenneth S. Geller. 2002. *Supreme Court Practice.* Eighth edition. Washington, D.C.: The Bureau of National Affairs, Inc.

Stolberg, Sheryl Gay and Charlie Savage. 2010. "Stevens's Retirement Is Political Test for Obama." *The New York Times*, April 9: A1.

Stras, David R. 2006. "The Supreme Court's Gatekeepers: The Role of Law Clerks in the Certiorari Process." *Texas Law Review* 85 : 1–58.

Stras, David R. 2007. "The Supreme Court's Gatekeepers: The Role of Law Clerks in the Certiorari Process." *Texas Law Review* 85 : 947.

Stumpf, Harry P. 1997. *American Judicial Politics*. Upper Saddle River, NJ: Prentice Hall.

Sungaila, Mary–Christine. 1999. "Effective Amicus Practice Before the United States Supreme Court: A Case Study." *Southern California Review of Law and Women's Studies* 8 187–195.

Tamanaha, Brian Z. 2006. *Law as a Means to an End: Threat to the Rule of Law*. Cambridge, UK: Cambridge University Press.

Tanenhaus, Joseph and et al. 1963. "The Supreme Court's Certiorari Jurisdiction: Cue Theory." In *Judicial Decision Making*, ed. Glendon Schubert. New York: Free Press, 111-131.

Tauber, Steven C. 1998. "On Behalf of the Condemned? The Impact of the NAACP Legal Defense Fund on Capital Punishment Decision Making in the U.S. Court of Appeals." *Political Research Quarterly* 51 (1): 191-219.

Taylor, John B. 1992. "The Supreme Court and Political Eras: A Perspective on Judicial Power in a Democratic Polity." *The Review of Politics* 54 (Summer): 345–368.

Thurber, James A. and Roger H. Davidson, ed. 1995. *Remaking Congress: Change and Stability in the 1990s*. Washington, D.C.: Congressional Quarterly Books.

Toobin, Jeffrey. 2005. "Swing Shift: How Anthony Kennedy's passion for foreign law could change the Supreme Court." *The New Yorker*, September 12.

Tushnet, Mark. 1995. "Policy Distortion and Democratic Debilitation: Comparative Illumination of the Countermajoritarian Difficulty." *Michigan Law Review* 94 (2): 245–301.

Ulmer, S. Sidney and David Willison. 1985. "The Solicitor General of the United States As Amicus Curiae in the U.S. Supreme Court, 1969–1983 Terms." Presented at the Annual Meeting of the American Political Science Association, New Orleans.

Ulmer, S. Sidney, ed. 1981. *Courts, Law and Judicial Processes*. New York: The Free Press.

Ulmer, S. Sidney, William Hintze, and Lois Kirklosky. 1972. "The Decision to Grant or Deny Certiorari: Further Consideration on Cue Theory." *Law and Society Review* 7 637–650.

Ulmer, S. Sidney. 1983. "Conflict with Supreme Court Precedents and the Granting of Plenary Review." *Journal of Politics* 45 474–478.

Ulmer, S. Sidney. 1984. "The Supreme Court's Certiorari Decisions: Conflict As a Predictive Variable." *American Political Science Review* 78 901–911.

Unah, Isaac, Ange, and Marie Hancock. 2006. "U.S. Supreme Court Decision Making, Case Salience, and the Attitudinal Model." *Law and Policy* 28 (3): 295–320.

Vanberg, Georg. 2000. "Legislative-Judicial Relations: A Game-Theoretic Approach to Constitutional Review." *American Journal of Political Science* 45 (April): 346-361.

Vose, Clement E. 1959. *Caucasians Only*. Berkeley: University of California Press.

Wahlbeck, Paul J., James F. Spriggs, and Forrest Maltzman. 1998. "Marshalling the Court: Bargaining and Accommodation on the United States Supreme Court." *American Journal of Political Science* 42 (Jan.): 294-315.

Wahlbeck, Paul. 1998. "The Development of a Legal Rule: The Federal Common Law of Public Nuisance." *Law and Society Review* 32 (3): 613–638.

Walker, Jack L., Jr., ed. 1991. *Mobilizing Interest Groups in America*. Ann Arbor: University of Michigan Press.

Wasby, Stephen L. 1984. "How Planned Is 'Planned Litigation'?" *American Bar Foundation Research Journal* 9 (Winter): 83–138.

Wasby, Stephen L., Anthony A. D'Amato, and Rosemary Metrailer. 1977. *Desegregation from Brown to Alexander: An Exploration of Court Strategies*. Carbondale, IL: Southern Illinois Press.

Wasby, Stephen L., Anthony A. D'Amato, and Rosemary Metrailer. 1976. "The Functions of Oral Argument in the U.S. Supreme Court." *Quarterly Journal of Speech* 62 (December): 410–422.

Wasby, Stephen L., ed. 1976. *Civil Liberties: Policy and Policy Making*. Lexington, MA: Lexington Books.

Wasby, Stephen L., Steven Peterson, James N. Schubert, and Glendon A. Schubert. 1992. "The Supreme Court's Use of Per Curium Dispositions: The Connection to Oral Argument." *Northern Illinois University Law Review* 13 : 1–32.

Wedeking, Justin. 2009. "Cognition and Decision Making of U.S. Supreme Court Justices." Presented at the 67th Annual National Conference of the Midwest Political Science Association, Chicago, IL.

Wedeking, Justin. 2010. "Supreme Court Litigants and Strategic Framing." *American Journal of Political Science* 54 (3): 617-631.

Wheeler, Stanton, Bliss Cartwright, Robert A. Kagan, and Lawrence M. Friedman. 1987. "Do the 'Haves' Come out Ahead? Winning and Losing in State Supreme Courts, 1870–1970." *Law & Society Review* 21 (3): 403–446.

Whissell, Cynthia and Lee Sigelman. 2001. "The Times and the Man as Predictors of Emotion and Style in the Inaugural Addresses of U.S. Presidents." *Computers and the Humanities* 35 255–272.

Whissell, Cynthia. 1989. "The Dictionary of Affect in Language." In *Theory, Research, and Experience*, ed. Robert Plutchik and Henry Kellerman. New York: Academic Press, 113–131.

Whittington, Keith E. 2005. "'Interpose Your Friendly Hand': Political Supports for the Exercise of Judicial Review by the United States Supreme Court." *American Political Science Review* 99 (November): 583-596.

Wiener, Frederick Bernays. 1954. "The Supreme Court's New Rules." *Harvard Law Review* 68 (Nov.): 20-94.

Wiggins, Stephen G. 1976. "Quasi-Party In the Guise of Amicus Curiae." *Cumberland Law Review* 7 : 293-305.

Wilson, Rick K. and Jane Sell. 1997. "'Liar, Liar…": Cheap Talk and Reputation in Repeated Public Goods Settings." *The Journal of Conflict Resolution* 41 (October): 695–717.

Wolfson, Warren D. 2002. "Oral Argument: Does It Matter?" *Indiana Law Review* 35 : 451.

Wolpert, Robin M. 1991. "Explaining and Predicting Supreme Court Decision-Making: The Gender Discrimination Cases, 1971–1987." Presented at the meeting of the Midwest Political Science Association, Chicago.

Wrightsman, Lawrence. 2008. *Oral Arguments Before the Supreme Court: An Empirical Approach*. New York: Oxford University Press.

Zeppos, Nicholas S. 1998. "Department of Justice Litigation: Externalizing Costs and Searching for Subsidies." *Law and Contemporary Problems* 61 (2): 171–190.

Zorn, Christopher. 1995. "Congress and the Supreme Court: Reevaluating the 'Interest Group Perspective'." Presented at the Annual Meeting of the Midwest Political Science Association, Chicago.

Zorn, Christopher. 2002. "U.S. Government Litigation Strategies in the Federal Appellate Courts." *Political Research Quarterly* 55 (1): 145–166.

Index